THE COMPANY WE KEEP

In Search of Biblical Friendship

Jonathan Holmes
Cruciform Press | September 2014

To Kelly, Scott, Nathan, and Joe: Your friendship
in my life has been an unexpected grace from God.
Thank you.

To Jennifer: Your friendship has been the single
greatest testimony to our Savior's sacrificial love.
I love you, friend.

– Jonathan Holmes

CruciformPress

"Jonathan Holmes has the enviable ability to say a great deal in a few words. Here is a wonderful primer on the nature of Biblical friendship—what it means and why it matters."

Alistair Begg, Senior Pastor, Parkside Church

"I talk with many Christians who have intensely practical questions about how to make and maintain friendships with their fellow believers. Jonathan Holmes' book is filled with answers that are equally down-to-earth, nitty-gritty, and specific. This book isn't just a roadmap for cultivating Christian friendship. It's also a tour guide, taking us where we need to go with warmth and wisdom."

Wesley Hill, Assistant Professor of Biblical Studies, Trinity School for Ministry; author of *Washed and Waiting: Reflections on Christian Faithfulness and Homosexuality*

"Jonathan Holmes has tackled an often neglected and sometimes misunderstood topic: biblical friendship. He brings clarity to what Christ-centered friendships are and how to cultivate them. In a time when friendships are defined by a few taps on a keyboard, this book will cause you to take pause and reflect on why and how God intended our friendships to be a testimony to a desperate world looking for intimacy in all the wrong places. Pick a friend, read this together, and watch how your faith and the faith of others grow as a result."

Dr. Garrett Higbee, author of *The Uncommon Community: Biblical Soul Care for Small Groups*; Board Member, Biblical Counseling Coalition

"Short. Thoughtful. Biblical. Practical. I'm planning to get my friends to read this book so we can transform our friendships into something more biblical. I am grateful to Jonathan Holmes for carefully helping us think through the topic of Christian friendships."

Deepak Reju, author; Pastor of Biblical Counseling and Families, Capitol Hill Baptist Church

"So often, books on biblical fellowship place our relationships in a "spiritual" realm where none of them really exist. Thankfully, Jonathan has succeeded in giving us a picture of how normal, daily, biblical friendships can be used by God to mold us into the likeness of Christ. He successfully steers clear of over-spiritualizing what friendship between brothers and sisters in Christ should look like. It is rich in its application of Scripture and practical in the way it connects all of our relationships to Christ. If you want a solid, fresh way of re-thinking all of your relationships, read this book."

Dr. Tim S. Lane, President, Institute for Pastoral Care; conference speaker; co-author of *Relationships: A Mess Worth Making* and *How People Change*

"Thought provoking, rooted in theology, and a topic that has needed to be addressed more deeply. I've often bemoaned the superficial relationships in the church so I'm thankful for a book that addresses this and takes gospel-saturated one-anothering seriously. I can assure you the church would be different and get the attention of the world if these types of friendships were pursued. I finished reading and wanted to invest more in Christ -focused relationships."

Dr. Ernie Baker, Professor of Biblical Counseling, The Master's College

"*The Company We Keep* presents a compelling vision of biblical friendship that glorifies Christ, builds up believers, and witnesses to the world. I was both encouraged and challenged in my own relationships and counseling ministry through the wisdom of this book. The section on friendship and same-sex-attraction is especially timely and helpful for the church today. Jonathan has written a clear, concise book that is biblically faithful, relationally practical, pastorally wise, and, above all, Christ-centered. I highly recommend it!"

Pat Quinn, Dir. of Counseling Ministries, University Reformed Church

"We live in a world of easy, quick, superficial, and selfish relationships where Christians need biblical wisdom about how to develop meaningful friendships. In *The Company We Keep* Jonathan Holmes provides this wisdom in abundant supply. This guide to biblical friendship is grounded in the timeless truth of God's Word, centered in the grace of Jesus Christ, and focused on relevant and practical application. This book is required reading for anyone desiring to grow in deeper Christian friendship."

Dr. Heath Lambert, Executive Director, The Association of Biblical Counselors

"*The Company We Keep* casts a vision for the kind of friendships we all really want—to love and be loved as Christ loves us. Jonathan provides practical guidance that is both biblical and inspiring. I'll be recommending this book to friends and counselees."

Winston T. Smith, faculty and counselor, Christian Counseling and Educational Foundation

"*The Company We Keep* is a refreshing and challenging book. Here you will find rich, practical, and theologically grounded counsel. Jonathan Holmes demonstrates that our need for friendship is rooted in the eternal relationships within the triune God in whose image we are created, illustrates how the self-centeredness of sin has distorted our view of friendship, and teaches us how to apply the humility of Christ to the intentional pursuit of careful relationships that draw attention to the gospel. This is a book that I wish had been available in my early years as a believer. I really need this book."

Paul Tautges, author; founder of Counseling One Another

"In *The Company We Keep*, Jonathan Holmes has made a significant contribution to the Kingdom. We expect far too little from our friendships, and Jonathan's work not only encourages us to expect more, it also equips us to give more. His four marks of biblical friendship—constancy, candor, carefulness, and counsel—provide a robust and relevant GPS for intentional and vulnerable gospel-centered friendships. The 'Dig Deeper' sections embedded in each chapter make this a great book not only for individuals, but also for small groups."

Robert W. Kellemen, Ph.D., author; Executive Director, Biblical Counseling Coalition

"People want to connect with others. It is part of the image of God in man. But so often we struggle to have meaningful relationships, settling instead for various kinds of cheap substitutes and wishing for more. In this work, Jonathan helpfully teaches a biblical theology of friendship and along the way he provides wise counsel while having his feet firmly planted in the reality that we have many God-given responsibilities. Wise will be the one who evaluates his own life and seeks to make practical changes to pursuing and enjoying true biblical friendships based on the conviction of the Holy Spirit."

Rob Green, Pastor of Counseling and Seminary Ministries, Faith Church

"*Friendship* is a word like *trust*. We all know what these words mean but we're not always sure how to 'do' them. Our tendency can be either to fear friendship or to deify what it means to have 'a good friend.' In *The Company We Keep*, Jonathan Holmes serves us well by giving us a functional definition, realistic expectations, and practical steps to develop the kind of biblical friendships God intended for his people."

Brad Hambrick, Pastor of Counseling, The Summit Church; author of *Burnout: Resting in God's Fairness*

"Friendships are such an important part of our lives, but there is so much confusion about what a true friend is. Is it someone I shop with, someone I play sports with, someone I meet for lunch, or someone I call when I'm in trouble who never condemns me? Jonathan winsomely unpacks what biblical friendship really is. Prepare to be blessed, encouraged, and perhaps surprised. Then look forward to putting his wise words into practice and enjoying sweet fruit. I wish all friendships had the focus Jonathan describes."

Amy Baker, Biblical Counselor, Faith Church

"Ever get the sense there's something lacking in your friend-ships? This book provides Christ-centered, practical wisdom on the obstacles and benefits of biblical friendships. You'll gain valuable direction for real-life relationships and you will see the vital role of biblical friendships as a witness to the gospel. From his wealth of experience as a biblical counselor, Jonathan Holmes knows that friendships can be hard but also deeply fulfilling, especially when pursued with an eye to God's glory."

Dr. Stephen K. Moroney, Professor and Chair of the Department of Theology, Malone University

"I loved this book because it honestly addresses a significant problem we all face in ways that are both theologically robust and delightfully practical. I especially appreciated Jonathan's authenticity as he described ways he has struggled with these very same concepts. I felt like I was talking to a good friend as I read the book—how appropriate for a book on friendship. Now I plan to get to work applying the tremendous principles I've read. I needed this."

Steve Viars, author; Senior Pastor, Faith Church

"In a world where we are seemingly surrounded by friends, many continue to search for meaningful friendships. *The Company We Keep* not only provides a theological lens to view friendship accurately, but gives practical insights on how to develop them in everyday life. This book will encourage and enhance your friendships from a biblical perspective to become what they are truly designed to be."

Joe Keller, D.Min., Vice President of Student Life, The Master's College

"We hear a lot about the goodness of marriage, the honor of parenting, and the call to disciple others, but so little about life's most common relationship: friendships. And what we see today is that like never before people have more connections and fewer true friends. My life receives so much richness thanks to Jonathan's friendship, and I believe yours will too by embracing what he has to say here. I challenge you not to read this book alone, but with a friend!"

Scott Zeller, Training Coordinator, Redeemer Church of Dubai

"I am glad that this book has been written. This short book challenges readers to understand God's bigger purpose in giving friendships. It is filled with biblical wisdom, honest reflections, and helpful questions. I highly recommend this book."

Lilly H. Park, Assistant Professor, Crossroads Bible College

"Jonathan Holmes has gifted the body of Christ with a fresh, insightful, relevant, and theologically-rich window into biblically-shaped, Christ-centered friendship. He invites the reader on an exploration, discovery, and practical pathway to healthy friendship. Not only does he unpack the relational challenges that can exist within friendships, but he also provides wisdom, direction, and hope for those desiring to experience friendships that thrive. This book is a timeless resource that could equip every reader on his or her journey to relating biblically."

Dwayne R. Bond, Ph.D., Lead Pastor, Wellspring Church

"With convicting transparency, Jonathan Holmes not only addresses the philosophical and motivational underpinnings of biblical friendships, he offers help in overcoming a lost obedience with practical applications. Helpful and penetrating questions accompany each chapter, making this book a useful tool for leaders and groups as they take on the challenge of deepening their commitment to bucking the cultural tendency to call shallow relationships 'biblical friendship.' Ideally, this book should not to be read alone, but along with people willing to take a deeper plunge into the challenge of biblical friendship.

With candor and insight, Jonathan exposes our sinful impediments to biblical friendships in a Christ-centered, contemporary manner. This book challenges those are maturing in their biblical friendships to continue to grow, and introduces others to the concepts and challenge of biblical friendships. Thus, fresh challenges, motivations, and applications to the common and pervasive problem of shallow or selfish relationships can be applied by those new to the faith as well as those who have been struggling to deepen relationships biblically for a long time."

Greg Cook, D.Min, Pastor, Christ Chapel Church

"With meaningful friendships in sharp decline in an age of superficial acquaintances, we receive encouraging words in *The Company We Keep*. In this book, Jonathan Holmes paints friendship in exalted hues, drawing inspiration from no less than the 'friendships' formed within the triune Godhead. When we image the sacrificial love of heaven, we create friendships on earth that bring great glory to God and immense delight to ourselves. This concise book is biblical and personal, incisive and emotive, theological and practical—and causes us to yearn for the prize of Christ-centered friendships. *The Company We Keep* elevates interpersonal relations to new heights, beyond fellowship to friendship."

Tim Savage, Ph.D., Senior Pastor, Camelback Bible Church

"*The Company We Keep* offers a beautiful invitation to participate in the life God has called us to live with one another. Throughout this short yet thoughtful and robust treatise on biblical friendship, I found myself stirred in different ways— excited with a renewed vision, convicted about my tendencies to 'go it alone,' and compelled to persevere in my fight to love and be loved. I also found myself drawing near to Jonathan, with his gentle tone and keen insights, as he brought us along on his own personal journey. I confidently recommend this work, which will serve the church well."

Robert K. Cheong, author; Pastor, Sojourn Community Church

"It is one thing for a church or an individual to be friendly, and quite another for us or our churches to be places where we find and make real friends. Jonathan's book helps us understand what real friendship is, and then how we can cultivate it in our lives and churches on God's terms. *The Company We Keep* is honest, realistic, and God-centered."

Sam Williams, Professor of Counseling, Southeastern Baptist Theological Seminary

"Yes! A book on a subject that all kinds of people—parents and grandparents, teenagers and empty nesters—often struggle with: biblical friendship. I will put this well-written, biblically saturated, easily accessible resource into the hands of as many church members as possible. This resource will inform, convict, and encourage people to pursue meaningful Christian friendship. Thank you, Jonathan, for living out these very principles in our friendship. May others benefit from this work."

Kelly Wright, Associate Pastor, Castleview Baptist Church

CruciformPress

<u>Our Books:</u> Short and to the point—about 100 pages.
Clear. Concise. Helpful. Inspiring. Easy to read.
Solid authors. Gospel-focused. Local-church oriented.

<u>Multiple formats:</u> Print and the three top ebook formats.

<u>Consistent Pricing:</u> Every title the same low price.

<u>Website Discounts:</u>

Print Books (list price $9.99)

1-5 Books	$8.45 each
6-50 Books	$7.45 each
More than 50 Books	$6.45 each

Ebooks (list price $7.50)

Single Ebooks	$5.45 each
Bundles of 7 Ebooks	$35.00
Ebook Distribution Program	6 pricing levels

<u>Subscription Options:</u> If you choose, print books or
ebooks delivered to you on a schedule, at a discount.

Print Book Subscription *(list $9.99)*	$6.49 each
Ebook Subscription *(list $7.50)*	$3.99 each

The Company We Keep: In Search of Biblical Friendship

Print / PDF ISBN: 978-1-936760-95-4
ePub ISBN: 978-1-936760-97-8
Mobipocket ISBN: 978-1-936760-96-1

Table of Contents

FOREWORD

Could there be anything more important? When we reflect on our lives, they are measured not by our incomes or good works, but by our relationships—by our friendships. This is true for everyone.

What makes a child's day "good" is a friendship forged on the playground. What stands out from the din of our daily activity is the personal connection we had with a neighbor or even a salesperson. What rivets the thoughts of a dying billionaire are the regrets from relationships that were broken and the joys of the friendships that remain.

We are, after all, offspring of the Triune God who has always existed as a unity of three persons, and, in a move that remains stunning, he calls us friends, which is the very best of relationships. God actually draws us into that triune friendship as co-participants. Who could have imagined?

Ah yes, all good things come from God himself, and friendships, indeed, are among the great gifts that he gives us.

Your guide in this book will be Jonathan Holmes. Since he will be pointing to God and his wisdom on friendships, Jonathan will be in the background. But it just wouldn't be right to have an anonymous person guide you through the topic of friendships. So you will get to know him along the way. You will meet his youngest daughter Ruby, appreciate his friendship with his wife, and listen to his extended conversations with those who join his family on vacations or share a meal with him. Before you get to the end of the book, Jonathan will be a guide who is becoming a friend.

There are some people who feel like friends almost immediately. They are the ones who have nothing to hide. They listen and are moved by the things that move you. They engage in that wonderful back-and-forth that is natural to your best relationships. Jonathan is that kind of person. If you meet him face-to-face, you will consider him a friend. He is the ideal guide for this most important matter.

– Ed Welch, CCEF

One
WHAT IS BIBLICAL FRIENDSHIP?

The Definition and the Goal

At age 25, David was saved by Jesus as he heard the gospel regularly preached at a large, vibrant church. He's been a member for six months now and overall it's been wonderful. One thing is odd, though. He expected everyone here to be his best friends ever, and it hasn't worked out that way.

Ann was raised in her church. Her bubbly personality allows her to make personal connections easily. There are lots of people she loves seeing on Sunday, and she does feel love for them in Christ. Yet even after all these years she still struggles to form and maintain ongoing, fruitful Christian relationships that break into real life.

When Ben is at church, he tends to stew in his own insecurities. *All these people have busy lives. Am I just being selfish in wanting friends? Maybe I should just come to meetings, do my best to serve and glorify God, and go home.*

Lindsey is a high school sophomore who couldn't wait to meet other young people in her family's new church. What she found was a confusing collection of cliques within cliques. How could she ever make real friends here?

Armand and Julie wonder if something is wrong with their marriage. Although they are each other's best friends, they feel a lack of meaningful friendship in their lives, and they don't know how to pursue it.

Brittany is a junior in college. People comment on how connected she is through Facebook, Twitter, and her blog. She also helps the local campus ministry chapter plan social activities. While she is friends, in a way, with literally thousands of people, she is often disappointed when others don't pursue her and help out in tough times.

Tom thinks his relationships in the church are fantastic. He and his buddies make plans on Sunday and then get together during the week to watch sports, play video games, and just hang out. He's grateful to God for these guys and he's sure that what they're enjoying has got to be about as good as it gets.

Damian loves to serve in church. Lately he's seen, however, that when he's in "servant mode" people can turn into projects. Turns out you can't be close friends with a project.

Stephanie works in the home raising her three young kids. Her husband's job requires long hours, so they usually arrive at church frazzled and slightly late. She tries to connect with other young moms, but despite the occasional phone call and shared prayer request, she still feels like there's a wall between her and other moms.

Common Questions

These people may be fictional, but their stories are all too typical. Should a Christian's expectations for friendship differ from those of a non-Christian? Many of us harbor silent questions like some of these:

- *If a group of people are all saved and adopted into God's family, then really—why can it seem so hard to form open, honest, genuine friendships in the church?*
- *Didn't Jesus say believers can be recognized by their love for one another? What is that supposed to look like? Whatever it is, why don't we see more of it?*
- *None of my church friendships really get much below the surface, but we enjoy them anyway. What's wrong with just keeping that status quo?*
- *Should it concern me that there's still no one in my church who actually knows me well?*
- *Will I ever have people in my life who truly accept me for the mess that I am? Or is it unrealistic and selfish of me to want that?*
- *What are normal expectations for biblical friendship? What should I be hoping for, and how can I get there?*

Some of these questions may feel familiar. Deep and meaningful friendships don't come easily—even within the church, and sometimes *especially* within the church. And because from time to time we all sense that things ought to be different, we can find the challenges of biblical friendship perplexing, frustrating, and discouraging.

It doesn't have to be this way.

Beyond Fellowship

Not every church has the same friendship "climate." A strong culture of fellowship within a church can help minimize the sense of isolation faced by individual believers. But I'm distinguishing here between *Christian fellowship* and *biblical friendship*.

Fellowship might be described as that special sense of companionship and love among believers based on our unity in Christ. This is a truly wonderful thing and can pave the way to the development of biblical friendships. But in this book I want to help you see what Christian fellowship can look like when taken to the next level and applied more personally. This is fellowship that has been given added depth, refinement, and detail through active investment in one another's lives. It's what I'm calling biblical friendship.

While some books for Christians have a chapter on the subject, the topic of friendship among Christians has been largely overlooked in recent years. Pastor and author Kevin DeYoung agrees, writing "It [friendship] is the most important-least talked about relationship in the church."[1] This is why I want to try to show you God's great design for biblical friendship and describe how we can all take concrete steps toward the kind of friendships that can and should exist among believers. As we begin our journey together, the first thing we need to grasp is how we came to have this legitimate need for biblical friendship.

The Origin of Relationships in the Community Known as God

In Genesis 1:26 God says, "Let us make man in our image, after our likeness." This surprising "us," right there near the start of Scripture, is only the first of many indications that our creator exists himself as one God in three persons.[2] Indeed, the eternal Trinity is the most fundamental expression of community and relationship. Therefore, one of the simplest yet most profound aspects of mankind being made in God's image is that we were designed to live in relationships.

As if to affirm that truth, the author of Genesis soon goes on to tell us, "Then the LORD God said, 'It is not good that the man should be alone; I will make a helper fit for him.'" (Genesis 2:18). Just as the "us" was surprising, this "not good" can likewise raise a reader's eyebrows. Up until now we have been told that *everything* God creates is good, yet suddenly he announces something about the created order is *not* good: it is *not good* Adam is alone. Why?

We see the answer in the solution God provided—a final creation. God causes Adam to fall asleep and creates for him Eve, a fellow human being, a woman and a friend. Some may say the creation of Eve is more about giving Adam a helpmate, but pastor and commentator R. Kent Hughes expands on the significance of this creation, "While [Genesis 2:18] relates directly to the creation of Eve, it is also a primary ontological statement about the nature of man, who is, whether he admits it or not, a relational being. His growth and significance are worked out in relationships."[3]

The "problem" of Adam being alone, therefore, did not reflect a failure either in Adam's divine design or in his performance as a person. It lay in the limited nature of humanity, that none of us can be a community in ourselves the way God is a community in himself. Adam *needed* community in order to better image the God who *is* a community. He was created to pursue, develop, and maintain human relationships as an integral part of being made in the image of the triune God. In the language of software programmers, Adam's "problem" prior to Eve was a feature, not a bug. As Tim Keller explains,

> This is one ache [the ache for friendship] that is part of [Adam's] perfection…God made us in such a way that we cannot enjoy paradise without friends. God made us in such a way that we cannot enjoy our joy without friends. Human friends. Adam had a perfect quiet time every day, twenty-four hours, never had a dry one, and yet he needed [friends].[4]

Like Adam and all who have come after him, you and I were made for biblical friendship. Even Jesus, the Second Adam, needed and desired friendship. Consistently in Jesus' earthly ministry, he sought the friendship and companionship of others. Scottish pastor Hugh Black explains, "He was perfectly human, and therefore felt the lack of friendship."[5] Whether it was twelve disciples of random backgrounds or a family like that of Lazarus,

Mary, and Martha, friendship was an indispensable element of Jesus' earthly ministry.

What we learn from these crucial first two chapters in Genesis, then, is that God has made man in his image. And part of our image-bearing capacity entails living in relationships with others—not relationships built merely around common interests, but relationships that emanate from our very nature as image bearers.

Here is the significance of Genesis 1–2: we reflect God's image when we live in God-centered *relationship*; when we pursue biblical *friendship*.

Sin, Shame, and the Breakdown of Relationships

But as we know, the storyline quickly goes awry when, in Genesis 3, Adam and Eve fall into temptation and sin enters the world. Immediately their perfect communion, which mirrored their perfect union and communion with God, is shattered.

Running and hiding, Adam and Eve isolate themselves from their Creator. God comes along in the cool of the day looking for his image-bearers and calls out, "Where are you?" Adam's response is painfully revealing. In his desperate scramble to justify himself, we see how quickly the union and fellowship he enjoyed with Eve has been lost. Gone is the transcendent, ecstatic, exultant song that rang through the garden when he first saw her: "This at last is bone of my bones and flesh of my flesh" (Genesis 2:23). Instead, Genesis 3:10 reads like a chattering string of futile self-justifications.

> *I* heard the sound of you in the garden, and
> *I* was afraid, because
> *I* was naked, and
> *I* hid myself

As soon as sin appeared, *we* quickly became *I*, and human history has never been the same.[6]

Just like every other aspect of the fall, Adam's sin has deeply corrupted our ability to pursue and maintain friendship with others. Not knowing any world except this fallen one, you and I can't begin to imagine just how true that is. The connection between our sin and our friendships has at least three components:

- A vertical component (the root cause)
- A motivational component (the internal result)
- A missional component (the external result)

Vertical

Paul describes our unredeemed state in Colossians 1:21 as one of alienation from God, hostility toward God, and sinfulness against God. If this fundamental vertical isolation between us and God is not addressed, then the ability to move horizontally toward others in biblical friendship is impossible. Thankfully, the good news of the gospel proclaims that we can be made right in our relationship and friendship with God because of the atoning work of his son, Jesus Christ.

Even after becoming Christians, however, sin continues to hinder our vertical relationship with him who saved us. Throughout our lives, our sin nature

continues to press us toward relational isolation, separa-
tion, and alienation from God, as well as from one another.
Thus, our ongoing vertical problem (with God) leads to
two horizontal problems (with others), problems that are
motivational and missional in nature.

Motivational

The reformer Martin Luther noted that sin curves us
inward. Left unaddressed, sin causes us to become
increasingly self-focused. This affects our motivations,
especially as we pursue others in friendship. Remember
the picture of Adam in the garden? He was looking for
someone to serve as an adequate companion in reflecting
the glory of God. Zebras could not do it. Elephants could
not do it. But a fellow human being and friend could.

Flash forward to the present, and we see how sin has
affected our pursuit of friends. It taints our motivations
before we even pursue someone else.

Do they like me?
Can I make them like me?
Will they accept me?
Will they love me?
What will they give to me?
What are they expecting from me?
Will they hurt me?

These questions are not inherently bad or evil, but
notice how they are all utterly self-referential. Me, me,
me—God and his purposes are woefully absent. In other
words, due to the inward-curving effects of sin, we often
pursue friendship not out of a biblical understanding of

bearing God's image and glorifying his all-encompassing gospel, but out of a desire for personal benefit.

Then, once our vertical problem has created an internal, motivational problem, it's inevitable we will have an external, missional problem.

Missional

Friendship has the power and ability to tell a story—and biblical friendship can tell a story that demonstrates that God came to us in Christ to redeem us for himself. Indeed, as we will discuss later in this book, the ultimate purpose and design of friendship is to point to God and his glory.

Yet sin can quickly make friendship about us, to the exclusion of God. When a non-Christian peers into our friendships, is he or she able to see the outlines of the gospel story, the good news of Jesus Christ? When our friendships exist for our own pleasure, comfort, and relational happiness, rather than a communication of God's love and mercy in the gospel, we're telling the story badly, and we may be telling the wrong story altogether.

Beyond the Fall

We see from Genesis 3 how sin affects our ability to be in friendship with one another. From that point the storyline continues downhill. In Genesis 4, Adam and Eve's son Cain murders his younger brother Abel in jealousy and rebellion. In just two chapters we have moved from a magnificent vision of loving relationships and intimate friendship to the petty, cold-blooded murder of a sibling.

Fast-forward to the New Testament. Into this mess

of broken relationships, God sends his one and only Son to reconcile and redeem a people for himself. Through his perfect life and righteousness, Jesus stands *in* our place, condemned *for* our sin, thus paving the way to the Father for all who will believe and confess his name. Mankind, once hopelessly alienated and separated from God because of sin, can now be brought near to God through his perfect Son, Jesus.

We are stunned to hear Jesus' words to the disciples in John 15:13–15, "Greater love has no one than this, that someone lay down his life for his friends. You are my friends if you do what I command you. No longer do I call you servants, for the servant does not know what his master is doing; but I have called you friends."

Let that sink in. Jesus calls you his friend.

This is more than enough to overflow our hearts. The One in whom the fullness of God dwells calls you and me *friends*. The One who became flesh and dwelt among us, living a perfect life on our behalf, calls you and me *friends*. Jesus, through his death on the cross, be-*friends* us so we can now go and *be* friends with others. I love how Steve Timmis puts it, "At the cross, the Godhead's friendship was ruptured so that our friendship could be restored."[7] The eternal communion, fellowship, and friendship, which the Godhead enjoyed for eternity past, were temporarily broken at the cross. In that breaking, as God poured out his wrath on Jesus, he restored the friendship that had been broken by our sin.

This is what makes biblical friendship distinct from the world's sentimental approximations: Jesus at the center. For not only is he the center, he also gives us the power to follow his example and befriend others. This embodied friendship, centered on Jesus, flows out into every area of life. Friendship ceases to be primarily something we *do*, and instead it transforms into something we *become* as we follow Christ.

When we embody biblical friendship, we bear Jesus' image, his character, his priorities, and his glory. No longer will our friendships be situated merely around common circumstances or interests, but will instead become an embodied commitment to live out the image of God together in every area of our life.

In his *Confessions,* the great theologian Augustine writes of a dear friend he had before he came to faith in Christ. Although Augustine and his friend were very close, he makes the distinction that true friendship must have Christ at the center, "No friends are true friends unless you, my God, bind them fast to one another through that love which is sown in our heart by the Holy Ghost, who is given to us."[8]

Centuries later, a Cistercian monk, Aelred of Rievaulx, would echo this when he wrote his famous treatise on friendship, "And so in friendship are joined honor and charm, truth and joy, sweetness and good-will, affection and action. And all these take their beginning from Christ, advance through Christ, and are perfected in Christ."[9]

Following in Augustine and Aelred's footsteps, Keller argues forcefully as well for Christ-centered friendship,

Friendship is only possible when there is a common vision and passion…For believers in Christ, despite enormous differences in class, temperament, culture, race, sensibility, and personal history, there is an underlying commonality that is more powerful than them all. This is not so much a "thread" as an indestructible steel cable.[10]

Augustine, Aelred, and Keller all recognize this transcendent element of a biblically shaped and embodied friendship: it all flows from our faith in Christ.

Biblical Friendship Defined

So then, for the purposes of this book, what do I actually mean when I use the phrase "biblical friendship"? In the fewest possible words, I mean that biblical friendship is explicitly Christ-centered. Here's the same idea, with a bit more elaboration:

Biblical friendship exists when two or more people, bound together by a common faith in Jesus Christ, pursue him and his kingdom with intentionality and vulnerability. Rather than serving as an end in itself, biblical friendship serves primarily to bring glory to Christ, who brought us into friendship with the Father. It is indispensable to the work of the gospel in the earth, and an essential element of what God created us for.

I hope you find that both inspiring and at least a little bit intimidating. For the remainder of this book we will journey together to unpack biblical friendship: what it is not, what it looks like, how it is formed, what threatens it, and how to recognize if it's working.

We all know that even our best efforts at friendship can go wrong. We have all been burned, rejected, cast off, and ignored by people whom we would really like to know better. Sometimes, in the spirit of biblical friendship, our best efforts to be vulnerable and transparent only leave us more lonely and empty than before.

But let me encourage you to hear me out. Allow this book to round out and inform your understanding of biblical friendship. I believe that as we unpack biblical friendship together, your understanding of it can be richly expanded and your practice of it can be revolutionized.

As the first and most important step, be encouraged in your friendship with Jesus Christ. Our Savior died for you so he could call *you* a friend! He is *the* faithful friend, the supreme friend. So cry out to him. Ask for the ability to understand biblical friendship better, and as a result to receive the grace and courage to pursue others with a glad heart—even if your attempts at biblical friendship sometimes go unrequited. As we come to realize what biblical friendship really is, we can become far better at pursuing others, drawing them closer to Christ and the church, even as we grow in our ability to better open ourselves up to others.

Dig Deeper

1. How would you describe the difference between fellowship and friendship? What have you learned from this chapter that helps you distinguish the two?

2. In what ways can your friendships become more Christ-centered? What would that look like practically?

3. As you seek deeper, more biblical friendships, what are some fears or anxieties you have?

4. Write out a brief prayer of thanksgiving to God for befriending you through Jesus Christ.

Two
EVERYDAY SUBSTITUTES

The Limits of Common Grace

I hope you caught a glimpse of an expansive vision for Christ-centered friendships in the previous chapter. It really is a beautiful picture—created for community, you and I bear witness to our Creator when we pursue relationships and form biblical friendships. Our God himself lives and exists within community. Having been made in his image, we are also made for biblical friendship and community and are called to live out the reality of it in every aspect of our lives.

That's the vision. Unfortunately, reality typically paints a very different picture. Few of us regularly enjoy a kind of friendship that extends much beyond a narrow range of shared activities and interests. We have trouble even grasping that God's vision is for an embodied friendship that abounds in the ordinary details of life—laughing, working, worshiping, eating meals, sharing heartaches, and encountering trials...together. Biblical friendship is intended by God as an all-encompassing spiritual discipline that engages every aspect of who we are: how we think (cognition), feel (emotion), and act (volition). The biblical practice of friendship can be an embodied journey where together we progressively fulfill our calling as God's children.

This vision of friendship stands in stark contrast to the status quo. Take even a casual look at the landscape of contemporary friendships and it's clear how far we are from the biblical intent. Friendships in our time are easily disposed of and easily forgotten. Typically costing us little and centering around little more than a shared interest, they can evaporate like morning mist.

Relationships in a Genesis 3 World

In a world broken and twisted by sin, we see all around us how quickly we settle for relational substitutes. We are easily deceived into believing the promises the culture makes in this area—promises that rich, warm, fulfilling relationships can follow quickly and easily as long as we both like (or "like") the same things. There are three substitutes we frequently take for the real thing: social media friendships, specialized friendships, and selfish friendships. All three are common in our culture, and they can combine and overlap in all sorts of ways. Because of God's common grace, relationships built on these substitutes might even thrive for a time, but they all fall woefully short of God's purposes for true friendship

The Social Media Friendship

It was 3:35 a.m. I had just woken up to the cries of my 11-month-old daughter, Ruby. She has a favorite pastime lately of waking up in the middle of the night just to see if you'll talk with her, change her diaper, or feed her an extra bottle. It is often hard for me to fall back to sleep once I get her back down, so I do what many other people do: I check all my social media accounts and email.

You know what happens next. By the time I read the blogs in my Feedly account, heart the adorable photos on Instagram, catch up with people on Facebook, watch the latest videos on Vine, and check out the latest news and quotes from Twitter, it is now a ridiculously early 4:42 a.m. Where in the world did the last hour go? Why was I not sleeping?

For many of us, the influence of social media has created a new category of relationship, a kind of "friendship" bearing little resemblance to the biblical ideal. Sherry Turkle writes, "Technology proposes itself as the architect of our intimacies. These days, it suggests substitutions that put the real on the run."[11] And these substitutions are not even especially satisfying—for all of the conveniences and advances in technology that purport to "connect" us, loneliness and depression persist.[12]

On the one hand, every human being was built for intimacy and relationship, yet through sin we have a penchant for looking for these things in all the wrong places. Email and Facebook and Twitter and all the rest, which promised to make relationships easier, often function as relational substitutes. The inherent promises of Facebook—that you can be connected to everyone, be friends with everyone—quickly leave their users disenchanted and even depressed.

"In the silence of connection," writes Turkle, "people are comforted by being in touch with a lot of people—carefully kept at bay. We can't get enough of one another if we can use technology to keep one another at distances we can control: not too close, not too far, just right."[13] This begins to get to the core of the problem: our sinful desire for control. We want friendships on our timetable, our terms of agreement. We do not want friendships that would move us out of our comfort zone.

Others are noticing the effects of social media on friendship as well. Technology journalist Nicholas Tuffnell observes:

> On a slightly deeper note, there's something about the relentless happiness of people on Facebook that I find monstrous. Everyone is apparently always somewhere better than I am and what's more, they're having a brilliant time. My life is not like that. In reality, no one's life is like that, these are of course constructed narratives, our "best ofs"—but sometimes it's hard to reason to yourself that these people aren't having fun all the time when all you ever see of them is pictures of them having fun all the time. I suddenly start to feel pangs of inadequacy and jealousy… and these people are supposed to be my friends.[14]

Tuffnell succeeds in exposing the grand lie of Facebook and other social media sites. While they promise connection and friendship, they often produce the exact opposite. Yet many of us continue to invest inordinate amounts of time into these sites, hoping they will deliver as promised. Like a government program gone bad, we try to convince ourselves that if we will only go a little bit further, this path we're on is sure to take us where we want to go—we just need more of the same. And if this month's hot new social media site can't deliver, surely the next one will...won't it?

The bent of the human soul is always to seek out meaning and significance in relational substitutes. Turkle sees through these and uncovers the underlying dynamics, "Technology is seductive when what it offers meets our human vulnerabilities. And as it turns out, we are very vulnerable indeed. We are lonely but fearful of intimacy. Digital connections and the sociable robot may offer the illusion of companionship without the demands of friendship."[15]

In case you were getting concerned, let me just say that at no point in this book will I suggest that you de-activate your Facebook account and abandon your Twitter handle. But I do hope, among other things, that we will all pause and reflect on the role of social media in our lives and the actual value of what these sites and apps provide us.

The Specialized Friendship

If the social-media friendship is willing to sacrifice intimacy and vulnerability for the illusion of companionship, then the specialized friendship is content to reduce a relationship down to a common activity or interest.

As human beings, we have a high capacity to compartmentalize not only our lives, but also our friends. I typically see friendships break into one of two categories: the "stage-of-life" friendship or the "common interest" friendship.

Stage of life. In the "stage-of-life" friendship, you simply surround yourself with people who are at a similar point in life. Everyone knows their lane and stays in it. College students with college students. Singles with singles. Young marrieds with other young marrieds. Mothers of preschoolers with other mothers of preschoolers. Senior saints with senior saints. And the list could go on.

I am in no way saying it is wrong to develop friendships within these various contexts. However, if you pursue these kinds of friendships to the exclusion of other opportunities, you're limiting the scope of what friendship can be and possibly letting the culture define your perspective. God intends for our best friendships to flow out of our relationship with Jesus Christ, not primarily our social demographics.

Common interest. In the "common interest" specialized friendship we section ourselves off according to a shared interest, hobby, or area of ministry. These are the common denominators of many a friendship, and understandably so. Again, I am not saying these types of friendships are utterly false or useless. But as a rule they fall short of what God has to offer us in friendship and ought not to be confused with biblical friendship. After all, biblical friendship is ultimately grounded in the greatest and most wonderful common denominator of all, a shared faith in Jesus Christ. This is why biblical friendship does not automatically discriminate based on the lesser common denominators that most worldly friendships are built around.

I have to remind myself of this on a regular basis. Not being a sports fan (the only organized sport I ever played was tee ball in Kindergarten), there are *lots* of conversations between men in our church I can't contribute to. That particular area of bonding so common among guys simply isn't open to me.

But that's far from the end of the story. Even though I serve on a pastoral team with a dozen men who all enjoy watching and playing sports, our friendship never suffers just because I *don't* share that area of interest. Why? Because our friendship is not limited to or even based on sports—it is grounded on the bedrock of faith in Jesus Christ and his kingdom rule.

Something similar to the "sports divide" can happen among women. Many women live at opposite ends of the spectrum in terms of personality and disposition. For example, some enjoy and have a gift for planning events and hosting parties, while others are terrified of anything more involved than having someone over for dessert. Some women love to go out for coffee together while others prefer connecting while running errands or attending the same playgroup. Sometimes women with one preference don't think they can relate to anyone with a different preference. But a healthy perspective on the true nature of biblical friendship allows people with different strengths and preferences to form deep and meaningful relationships that transcend any of these secondary factors.

The Selfish Friendship

Finally, the selfish friendship seeks friendship purely for what can be gained for the all-important Me. Out of the three friendship substitutes, this is the most sinister.

I may try to befriend you because I believe that your friendship would give me status or raise my public profile. Maybe I want a friend who feeds my desires to be flattered and complimented. Whatever the specific reason, this kind of friendship is essentially a transaction: What can I give you in exchange for something I want? In an obsessively materialistic society like ours, these kinds of friendships form the backbone of nearly all business relationships. This conditions us to see them as normal and sets the stage for non-business relationships to emulate them. For many of us, and not just among non-Christians, the selfish friendship has largely taken over.

If a biblical friendship is essentially one that is Christ-centered, it's hard to imagine a worse counterfeit than a friendship that is self-centered.

Disenchantment, Idolatry, and Diminished Humanity

Social media friendships, specialized friendships, selfish friendships—each one is like wax fruit in a bowl. They might look good, but most of us eventually discover that the appeal doesn't run very deep. We can then become disenchanted with friendship in general, and discouraged that things can really get any better. As a result, we wall ourselves off from an area of life that God intends us to cultivate for his glory. Either that, or out of desperation we try to force our less-than-biblical relationships to provide satisfaction, heavily re-reinvesting ourselves in them and turning them into an idol.

In James 1:13–15, we see the internal progression of any form of sin. James lists out the stages of falling into sin: temptation, allurement, enticement, and finally death. As we have seen, Satan is extremely adept at promising the better life through whatever means possible, and one way he does this is by making the pursuit of a friend the all-consuming directive and goal for life, to the exclusion of the pursuit of God.

Paul Tripp says that when we make a good thing into an ultimate thing, it becomes a bad thing. This can certainly apply to friendship. In the pursuit of friendship with others, we can neglect our primary calling to pursue Christ. The friendship we so ardently search for becomes our functional savior—a distraction from our boring life, an escape from loneliness, and a source of comfort in difficult times. Let me emphasize again: in God's grace and mercy, at times friendship can indeed be a source for all these things. As with any potential idol, it's a matter of degree. Until it becomes an ultimate thing, healthy friendship is a good thing.

Paul Tripp and Tim Lane refer to friendships that

have morphed into idols as "enmeshed" friendships, describing them this way, "Because [the two people] are so dependent on each other, they can be easily hurt when the other does not meet their needs. Because their expectations for the relationship are so high, they tend to live in isolation from other people…This kind of relationship is exhausting."[16] Over time these friendships die under the weight of expectation placed upon them—expectations that only can be realized and fulfilled in our relationship in Christ.

Novelist Jonathan Safran Foer, commenting on the effect of communication technologies on friendship, ends up illuminating a weakness found in all the relational substitutes I have been describing. These technologies began, of course, as legitimate and convenient *substitutes* for human relationship and activity. However,

> …a funny thing happened: we began to prefer the diminished substitutes. It's easier to make a phone call than to schlep to see someone in person. Leaving a message on someone's machine is easier than having a phone conversation—you can say what you need to say without a response; hard news is easier to leave; it's easier to check in without becoming entangled. So we began calling when we knew no one would pick up.
>
> Shooting off an e-mail is easier, still, because one can hide behind the absence of vocal inflection, and of course there's no chance of accidentally catching someone. And texting is even easier, as the expectation for articulateness is further reduced, and another

shell is offered to hide in. Each step "forward" has made it easier, just a little, to avoid the emotional work of being present, to convey information rather than humanity.

THE problem with accepting—with preferring—diminished substitutes is that over time, we, too, become diminished substitutes. People who become used to saying little become used to feeling little.[17]

I believe Foer has put his finger on the heart of the issue. Did you see it? Over time as we accept the substitute for the real, the fleeting friendship for the Christ-centered friendship, we ourselves lose some of our humanity. From the Christian perspective, we lose an opportunity to bear testimony to our Creator. We've taken a good thing—friendship built on social media or common interests—and hoped it would provide for us the same level of satisfaction as true relationship and friendship.

Seeing Friendship Rightly

In all of this, the Christian equipped with a biblically-shaped theology of friendship can understand technology, social media, and common interests for what they are—not more than they are, and not less—and thus place them in their proper framework. Technology, social media, and common interests are helpful *contexts* and *tools* to help *facilitate* friendship, but friendship itself is always more than these.

Truly biblical friendship is embodied in the Trinity, empowered by Jesus Christ, and intended as a spiritual discipline among God's people for the purpose of glorifying him. This is the heart of the matter—not hobbies and horticulture, sports and scrapbooking, but Jesus Christ.

Dietrich Bonhoeffer employed this theme in his book, *Life Together*, in which he made the point that true community and friendship must find its locus in Jesus Christ, not common interests or age affinities. He writes,

> Christianity means community through Jesus Christ and in Jesus Christ…we belong to one another only through and in Jesus Christ. What does this mean? It means, first, that a Christian needs others because of Jesus Christ. It means, second, that a Christian comes to others only through Jesus Christ.[18]

This is the enchanting, encouraging, and life-giving role of the gospel as it applies to this matter of friendship: you are brought into friendship by Jesus Christ in order to

1. pursue the lost for friendship ideally *leading to* Christ,
2. pursue fellow believers for friendship *grounded in* Christ.

If the everyday friendship substitutes are as impoverished and incomplete as I've described in this chapter, what should biblical friendship embody and look like? Does Scripture speak holistically to a biblical ethic of friendship? In the next chapter we will begin to explore these questions and discover that the answer to each of them is *yes*.

Dig Deeper

1. Consider your participation in social media. Do any changes, either in expectation or usage, need to take place? Why or why not?
2. Why do you think relational substitutes are easy replacements for friendship? How have you seen this happen in your own friendships?
3. Which of the three relational substitutes do you often find yourself falling into?

Three
THE MARKS OF BIBLICAL FRIENDSHIP

Constancy, Candor, Carefulness, and Counsel

For much of high school, I struggled to make friends. A self-acknowledged introvert, I faced the garden-variety struggles of seeking to fit in, desiring to be liked, and hoping to be accepted. Most of my friendships were cordial and warm, but largely superficial. So as it came time to leave for college, I faced a lot of angst at the prospect of starting all over again, trying to build relationships with an entirely new group of people.

My first year at college was a tough one. In spite of my introversion and self-consciousness, I was, like a lot of college kids, determined to reinvent myself — especially when it came to relationships. I centered my strategy on techniques. That is, I tried to be funny, spontaneous, and even easy-going. While these weren't exactly natural behaviors for me, they seemed like the ticket to my desired destination. As the school year finished out, however, I realized how exhausting it had all been. Was friendship supposed to be *this* difficult? In *The Four Loves*, C.S. Lewis describes what I was doing,

> That is why those pathetic people who simply "want friends" can never make any. The very condition of having Friends is that we should want something else besides Friends....Friendship must be about something...Those who have nothing can share nothing; those who are going nowhere can have no fellow travellers.[19]

It dawned on me that friendship isn't so much a series of things we need to *do*. Friendship is more about who we need to *be*.

This realization led to huge positive changes for me. For the rest of college I not only forged lasting friendships, but also met my best friend and future wife. Since then, I've come to learn that friendship flourishes best when we seek to *be* and *embody* the type of friend we see in God himself.

There is no better book in the Bible from which to glean wisdom about human relationships, and friendships in particular, than Proverbs. The writers of Proverbs are deeply interested in human relationships, because this is where wisdom is tested and worked out.

Drawing from this deep well of wisdom on human relationships, Pastor Tim Keller identifies from Proverbs four characteristics that distinguish wise friendships.[20] There may well be others, but these four can help us think concretely about biblical friendship:

- Constancy
- Candor
- Carefulness
- Counsel

These will be our focus for the rest of this chapter.

Constancy

If you know very much about the millennial generation, you aren't likely to say their friendships are characterized by constancy. Since the moment these young men and women were born, the very concept of friendship has become increasingly disposable and fleeting. Many in that generation will testify to the confusing friendship dynamics practiced by their peers. One day you're in, the next day you're out. One day you have a "best friend," the next day you don't. A "friend" is often someone who meets your needs or fits into your schedule—a matter of convenience.

The Proverbs push back against this fleeting view of friendship in the strongest of terms and portray truly biblical friendship as something constant and abiding. Proverbs 18:24 states, "But there is a friend who sticks closer than a brother." In an ancient Near Eastern culture, where family was everything, such a statement would have been provocative, to say the least. A friend can be closer to you than a biological brother? The wisdom of the Proverbs answers with a resounding Yes! In Proverbs 19:7, moreover, we are told that a poor man's brothers will hate him, pointing out that biological connection alone is no guarantee of faithfulness in adversity.

This constancy and consistency is further supported when the sage writes in Proverbs 20:6, "Many a man proclaims his own steadfast love, but a faithful man who can find?" There is a sense not only in Proverbs, but throughout the storyline of the Bible, that a true biblical friend can be depended on through good and bad times, in times of prosperity or adversity.

Look at the classic story of friendship between David and Jonathan. To be in friendship with David, Jonathan—not at all a blood relative of David's—at times risked his princely crown, his kingly inheritance, and even his life. Regardless of whether David was in or out favor with the often-murderous King Saul, his friendship with Jonathan, Saul's son, never wavered.

Scottish pastor William Arnot comments on the staying power of biblical friendship,

> Many will court you while you have much to give; when you need to receive, the number of your friends will be diminished, but their quality will be improved. Your misfortune, like a blast of wind upon the thrashed corn, will drive the chaff away, but the wheat will remain where it was. How very sweet sometimes is the human friendship that remains when sore adversity has sifted it.[21]

Isn't this what we long and hope for? A friendship which, when the waves and winds of adversity have "sifted" us, remains as faithful and abiding as ever?

It should not surprise us that this characteristic of

constancy ties back to our friendship with God. He is the one who is a constant and faithful presence in our lives. He is the friend who is a refuge in time of trouble and a shelter in time of storm.

For me, this mark of constancy brings to mind Frodo and Sam from Tolkien's *Lord of the Rings* trilogy. Popularized in film by director Peter Jackson, Sam and Frodo's journey to Mordor is a moving storyline of faithfulness and care. If you've seen the movies or read the books, you know that one of the keys to Frodo's success is the constancy of Sam's friendship. Several times, Frodo tries to carry the burden of the Ring and complete the journey to Mt. Doom alone, and yet each time Sam's persistence and faithfulness keep Frodo from deadly isolation. Sam will allow no adversity to come between him and his commitment to Frodo. Even when the wicked Gollum deceptively seeks to maneuver his way into position by defaming Sam's character, Sam remains constant and faithful to Frodo.

Indeed, the seeds of constancy are sown in the first book of the trilogy when Sam and the other hobbits entreat Frodo to make the journey collectively.

> You can trust us to stick to you through thick and thin—to the bitter end. And you can trust us to keep any secret of yours—closer than you yourself keep it. But you cannot trust us to let you face trouble alone, and go off without a word. We are your friends, Frodo. Anyway: there it is. We know most of what Gandalf has told you. We know a good deal about the

ring. We are horribly afraid—but we are coming with you; or following you like hounds.[22]

Biblical friendships are not fleeting and easily disposable, but are characterized by true constancy, in defiance of the obstacles continually tossed at us by the effects of the fall.

Candor

A second characteristic of a biblical friendship highlighted in Proverbs is candor. Framed in a biblical context, candor is the ability to speak truth in love for the good of your friend.

Proverbs 27:5–6 says, "Better is open rebuke than hidden love. Faithful are the wounds of a friend; profuse are the kisses of an enemy." It may seem like this doesn't make sense: wounds hurt; kisses feel good. Yet the Proverbs tell us a biblical friend is willing to wound us, and those wounds are actually for our good. This kind of constructive wounding, even via the pain of open rebuke, is shown to be a mark of true faithfulness, an expression of love that refuses to be hidden for the sake of convenience or a false sense of peace. Silence in the face of a brother or sister's folly is no act of love, but the wounds of correction *are*, however uncomfortable it may be to inflict them. (More on this in the next chapter.)

Proverbs 28:23 adds to the picture. "Whoever rebukes a man will afterward find more favor than he who flatters with his tongue." Once again, uncomfortable honesty wins out over the path of least resistance. One can infer from these proverbs that if you are unwilling to offend by speaking candidly in the context of a friendship, you probably are not being a biblical friend.

In *The Reformed Pastor*, Richard Baxter muses on the necessity of candor in friendships.

> We will take all things well from one that we know entirely loves us. We will put up with a blow that is given us in love sooner than with a foul word that is spoken to us in malice or in anger. If you be their best friends, help them against their worst enemies. And think not all sharpness inconsistent with love: parents correct their children, and God himself "chastens every son whom he receives."[23]

What do you suppose are the enemies Baxter says we should defend one another against? The classic three-fold enemy: the world, the Evil One, and our own flesh.

Nothing has played a more important role in my friendships than this kind of confrontation in love. One particularly vivid example for me involves a time I was stringing Christmas lights from our second-story bathroom window. As I leaned out the window into an unforgiving Northeast Ohio winter, my wife stood below offering one suggestion after another.

"Try moving the whole thing a little to the left."

"Okay, um, wait. I mean my left. So try moving them a little to the right."

"Could you come down and see what you think? I'm not sure."

All reasonable suggestions, and made with a perfectly good attitude. Yet I could feel my blood boiling. *Just figure out where you want the lights!* I thought. When the job was finished, I spent the rest of the evening storming around the house, trying to make it perfectly clear just how difficult it had been for me to hang those lights. Watching all of this was my good friend who had come to spend a few days with us.

The next morning as I drove my friend to the airport, he spoke these insightful words, "It seems like you are still struggling with a lack of patience and love toward your wife." The observation stung me deeply, because he was so obviously right. This friend knows me better than almost anyone, and he wasn't referring to just this one instance—he has seen me struggle in this area for years. Because of that he was able to come alongside me to speak with gracious candor.

He proved Charles Bridges' helpful words to be true:

What is the friend, who will be a real blessing to my soul? Is it enough that he will humour my fancies, and flatter my vanity? Is it enough that he loves my person, and would spend his time and energies in my service? This comes far short of my requirement. I am a poor straying sinner, with a wayward will and a blinded heart; going wrong at every step. The friend for my case is one, who will watch over me with open rebuke; but a reprover when needful; not a flatterer. The genuineness of a friendship without this mark is more than doubtful; its usefulness utterly paralyzed.[24]

Our friendship, despite distance, continues to be fruitful and a constant reminder of God's grace to me. My friend's faithful confrontation helps me become a better husband, a better father, a better child of God...a better friend.

A wise pastor once said that in life you'll have many fans and many foes, but few friends. French essayist Montaigne agrees, writing, "Those who venture to criticize us perform a remarkable act of friendship for to undertake to wound and offend a man for his own good is to have a healthy love for him."[25]

It was my friend's wounding, his willingness to speak truth in love, that God used in that instance to continue to help me grow in my journey towards Christlikeness. We need to be sure our friends have what Tim Keller calls, "hunting licenses" to enter into the dark spaces and secret gardens of our life to call us to holiness.[26] The willingness to engage in biblical candor for the sake of another's spiritual good is one way in which biblical friendship is obviously and dramatically different from those worldly substitutes that typically ignore unpleasant subjects.

Carefulness

A third mark of biblical friendship is carefulness. If candor suggests we need to be courageous in speaking into a friend's life, carefulness urges wisdom and consideration in *how* to live out the life of friendship. A biblical friend is careful, not in an overtly timid or cautious sense, but in consideration and care. A biblical friend should be full of care for his friend.

In three particular areas, the authors of Proverbs offer us a glimpse into how a friend should be careful: in his speech, in his timing, and in his stewardship.

Careful in Speech and Timing

I'm combining these two categories because in practice they so often coincide. *What* we say (the content) should quite often be influenced by *when* we say it (the circumstances). Proverbs 25:20 illustrates this well. "Whoever sings songs to a heavy heart is like one who takes off a garment on a cold day, and like vinegar on soda." Singing songs is often a good thing, but trying to spread joy to people who are currently grieving and hurting is worse than unhelpful; it's insensitive and unkind.

Proverbs 27:14 offers another accessible illustration, "Whoever blesses his neighbor with a loud voice, rising early in the morning, will be counted as cursing." I love mornings; the earlier the better. I enjoy getting up and starting my day with a workout, quiet time, and coffee. My wife, however, is *not* a morning person. Should I rouse her excitedly at 5 a.m., urging her to leap out of bed and seize the day for Jesus? Trust me, such an approach would be the antithesis of wisdom for both of us.

So how does a biblical friend ensure his words are like "apples of gold in a setting of silver" (Proverbs 25:11)? We need to match the content of our speech to the immediate circumstances—the timing element. But we also need to let what we say be informed by our level of knowledge. When we know someone extremely well, we are positioned to speak at a deeper level than when we know him or her only moderately well.

Can you see how each of these things integrate with and play off one another? The careful friend, wise about his timing, will know when and how to speak truth in love, and he will also know when his friend has had enough and needs time alone to process.

We should seek to tailor our words so they match the circumstances and the depth of our friendship. This requires prayerful discernment. Then, as friendship grows and develops, we must continue to engage in a faithful pursuit of the heart, thus emulating Jesus' knowledge and pursuit of us. This growing knowledge will help our words become ever more careful, considerate, and effective.

Careful in Stewardship

The biblical friend is also careful to steward the trust of friendship that has been granted to him. Solomon explains in Proverbs 11:13 that, "Whoever goes about slandering reveals secrets, but he who is trustworthy in spirit keeps a thing covered." Wise stewardship of a friend's trust is critical to the success of biblical friendship.

A biblical friend seeks no pleasure in unnecessarily revealing his friend's weaknesses, trials, hurts, and disappointments. If the venue and audience is appropriate (a complex topic I won't try to address here), then thoughtful and conscientious vulnerability is often warranted. But casual divulgence of the inner workings of a friend's heart and life is never appropriate.

Counsel

Biblical friendship is marked by constancy, candor, carefulness, and finally, wise counsel. Once again the Proverbs are replete with wisdom concerning the counsel of wise friends:

- Without counsel plans fail, but with many advisers they succeed (Proverbs 15:22).
- For by wise guidance you can wage your war, and in the abundance of counselors there is victory (Proverbs 24:6).
- Oil and perfume make the heart glad, and the sweetness of a friend comes from his earnest counsel (Proverbs 27:9).
- Iron sharpens iron, and one man sharpens another (Proverbs 27:17).

This mark of friends—counseling one another—is often absent from modern friendships, even in the church. But in a truly biblical friendship we desire to spur one another on into greater Christlikeness. Don't let the word *counseling* scare you away. *Counseling* is simply inter-personal ministry. It is living out the one-anothers of Scripture together. In a biblical friendship, counseling can and should thrive naturally. Pastor and author R. Kent Hughes writes,

> The deepest of friendships have in common this desire to make the other person royalty. They work for and rejoice in the other's elevation and achievements. There are no hooks in such friendships, no

desire to manipulate or control, no jealousy or exclu-
siveness — simply a desire for the best for the other.[27]

Too often our friendships lack this mark of godly
counsel that seeks to build one another up. Many men
like to surround themselves with drinking buddies, golf
partners, or gym friends. Women often form their friendships around dance practices, soccer games, scrapbook
parties, or Pinterest. It is rare to find friendships seeking a
higher goal than our own personal happiness and comfort.
What we need most in this area, however, are friendships
oriented for Christ's glory. Pastor Gordon MacDonald
writes,

> There is a certain "niceness" to a friendship where
> I can be, as they say, *myself*. But what I really need
> are relationships in which I will be encouraged to
> become *better than* myself. *Myself* needs to grow a
> little each day. I don't want to be the *myself* I was
> yesterday. I want to be the *myself* that is developing
> each day to be more of a Christlike person.[28]

What a stark contrast to the friendships of today!
We want friendship on our terms and conducive to
our comfort, and yet as McDonald helpfully reminds
us, biblical friendship is not just an endeavor toward
self-realization but a mutual journey toward Christlikeness. All of these marks — constancy, candor, care, and
counsel — empowered by the Holy Spirit, help separate and
distinguish biblical friendship from a crowd of counterfeits.

The Cappadocian fathers, Gregory of Nazianzus (329-389) and Basil of Caesarea (330-379) famously battled the Arian controversies of the fourth century together. Unknown to many was their intimate and strong friendship. In Gregory's lengthy *Funeral Oration* to Basil he said:

> In studies, in longings, in discussions I had him as companion....We had all things in common...But above all it was God, of course, and a mutual desire for higher things, that drew us to each other. As a result we reached such a pitch of confidence that we revealed the depths of our hearts, becoming ever more united in our yearning.[29]

Reading of a relationship like this, you can't help but think how rarely modern friendships reach this level. And at this point in the book, you may understandably be a bit overwhelmed—for in any friendship, who among us can consistently offer true constancy, candor, carefulness, and counsel?

The simple answer is: no one. But the fuller and more accurate answer is: no one *but* Jesus Christ. He is the perfect friend. All of these marks are perfectly fulfilled in him. In the ultimate act of friendship he laid down his very life for us, so he could call us *friends*. This is why to call another *friend* is no small praise, but the very essence of the Christian faith. Gregory of Nazianzus may put it best when he surmises, "If anyone were to ask me, 'What is the best thing in life?' I would answer, 'Friends.'"[30]

As I reflect on these marks of friendship, my heart overflows with thankfulness for the close friends God has graciously given to me, some at just the right moment. Recently I took my family on vacation with two close friends and their families. On our way to buy groceries for the week, I told them about this book and sought their feedback on what marks good friendship. Although we are living out biblical friendship with one another pretty well, we struggled to express the essence of our relationships in just a few words.

Yet over the balance of that week we shared every aspect of life together. We ate, talked, laughed, prayed, played, and enjoyed one another's company. The marks of constancy, care, candor, and counsel were all present in our interactions. In those moments, I never thought to myself, "Yes, this is the mark of constancy," or "You're counseling me right now!" Instead our friendships embodied and carried these distinguishing marks within the very fabric of our interactions.

For those who are seeking friendships like the ones described in Proverbs, do not despair or give up. In the next chapter we will go on to describe how friendship is forged and cultivated. It is one thing to acknowledge these marks of biblical friendship, but now let us discover how these marks become more of a reality in our current relationships.

Dig Deeper

1. In which of the four marks of friendship do you see your greatest strength?
2. In which area do you need to see Spirit-empowered growth?
3. Describe a time when a friend has displayed one of these particular marks of friendship. What was the effect on your friendship?

Four
THE FORGING OF BIBLICAL FRIENDSHIP

Making the Most of Your Time

We have just taken a look at four marks of biblical friendships: constancy, candor, carefulness, and counsel. Wonderful in theory, aren't they? But how does one actually get there?

To push back a little against the technique-obsessed, quick-fix spirit of the age, let me be clear that there aren't any overnight solutions. Like virtually everything else in the Christian life, change comes gradually. Biblical friendship is developed organically. It takes patience, commitment, and liberal applications of grace.

We are ultimately looking for something that I have been calling an *embodied friendship*, a friendship that really becomes part of you as you live it out over time. Our tendency, as I've said, is to reduce friendship to the occasional shared activity or interest. And while these are typically necessary to the development of biblical friendships, we have to be careful not to confuse them with the goal.

In *The Four Loves*, C.S. Lewis makes an insightful distinction. He notes how in the past, men in particular would have to come together to hunt, find food, and discuss survival strategies. Lewis maintains that this type of cooperation is best understood as companionship. He writes, "This Companionship is, however, only the matrix of Friendship. It is often called Friendship, and many people when they speak of their 'friends' mean only their companions. But it is not Friendship in the sense I give to the word."[31]

The "matrix of friendship"—I find that phrase helpful. Shared activities and interests create a frame or context for the formation of biblical friendship. Lewis goes on to differentiate further between shared-activity relationships ("Companionship") and something more like real friendship:

> Friendship arises out of mere Companionship when two or more of the companions discover that they have in common some insight or interest or even taste which the others do not share and which, till that moment, each believed to be his own unique treasure (or burden). The typical expression of opening Friendship would be something like, "What? You too? I thought I was the only one."[32]

Discovering unexpected common ground does seem to be a vital element in the forging of a genuine friendship.

I see this as shared interests taken to the next level. But even these deeper connections can shift and change over time, as seen in countless worn-out friendships that were once vital and strong.

So how can you sustain and deepen a friendship so it grows into a biblical friendship? The forging of biblical friendship all comes down to investing time wisely. This means having the right attitudes and the right goals, and then using conversation and context to facilitate those attitudes and serve those goals.

The Truth About Time

We all have the same hours in a day and we all make choices about what's important. Devotional life? Church activities? Family? Making a living? Staying healthy? Stewarding your possessions? Serving Christ and others? Getting enough rest?

How to juggle it all?

I don't have any simple answers to that increasingly complex question, but I do know this to be absolutely true: saying Yes to one thing means saying No to lots of other things. When it comes to setting the course of our own lives (to the extent we finite and fallen creatures can do this in a world with limited options), the most powerful tool available to us is the ability to say Yes to some things and No to everything else.

If we want biblical friendship, we must be willing to invest a resource that is limited and irreplaceable. We must invest our time.

Attitudes and Goals

Of course, investing time is not enough in itself. *How* and *why* we pursue biblical friendship is crucial. The right attitudes and goals are essential to forming and cultivating truly biblical friendships. To put it simply, biblical friendships are forged amidst a commitment to bring glory to God through this particular friendship.

Today, friendships often languish because there is no sense that the friendship exists other than to further common interests and mitigate personal loneliness. But the forging of truly biblical friendships requires a Christ-enabled commitment to love God and love one another, a commitment to pursue *Christ* and your friend's highest welfare *in Christ*.

Augustine in his *Letters* writes,

> There can be no full and true agreement about human things among friends who disagree about divine things, for it necessarily follows that one who despises divine things esteems human things more than he ought, and that whoever does not love God who made man, has not learned to love man rightly.[33]

Augustine goes on to recite the great commandment to love God with one's whole being and love one's neighbor as oneself.[34] He concludes his argument saying, "If you and your friend hold fast to these two commandments, your friendship will be true and eternal, uniting you not only to each other but to the Lord himself."[35]

This brings wonderful clarity to the attitudes and

goals that ought to be associated with the development of biblical friendship. When we rightly love God, it orients and orders our love for others. Our friendship with others does not become higher than our love for God, but flows out of that love. Biblical friendship draws its strength from a divine and inexhaustible source. It ultimately works to further the glory of him who built into us a longing for both divine and human friendship. Biblical friends seek more than the friendship itself. In effect, the friendship is put into service for God's glory.

The cultivation of a shared faith in Christ for the good of one another and the glory of God can serve as the lasting bedrock of biblical friendship. Only God's divine, unchanging nature can provide the foundation necessary for friendships to be built, forged, and cultivated. Consider David and Jonathan, Ruth and Naomi, Paul and Luke—were these friendships simply built on common interests or endeavors? No, something much deeper was at work. God was at the center.

As you seek to pursue biblical friendship, I encourage you to make these attitudes and goals explicit. This doesn't mean every conversation in the context of a biblical friendship has to pivot tightly around God's ongoing work of redemption in our lives and in the world. Nor does it mean every biblical friendship needs to look exactly the same, for God made each of us to be in some ways unique. At the same time, if the open acknowledgment of these attitudes and goals is not a touchstone of your friendship, you may be straying away from the cultivation of a genuinely biblical friendship.

Conversation and Contexts

Ours is a faith in which words are inescapably central. God reveals himself to us in the Scriptures through words. The gospel is communicated one person to another through words. We sing and pray to God using words. We encourage one another in the faith through words. In the end, therefore, so much of building biblical friendships comes down to conversation.

Shared activities are indeed invaluable. These can include meals, church events, hospitality, acts of service, entertainment, celebrations, sports and exercise, and more. While these kinds of shared activities can certainly build relationships through nonverbal means, they also provide a context for conversation—another opportunity to talk.

One of my favorite poems is Robert Frost's "A Time to Talk."

> When a friend calls to me from the road
> And slows his horse to a meaning walk,
> I don't stand still and look around
> On all the hills I haven't hoed,
> And shout from where I am, What is it?
> No, not as there is a time to talk.
> I thrust my hoe in the mellow ground,
> Blade-end up and five feet tall,
> And plod: I go up to the stone wall
> For a friendly visit.[36]

If we want to *have* biblical friendships, we need to *be* people who relish the opportunity simply to talk. Ask yourself, *Can I really expect to have a decent friendship of any kind—much less a biblical one—with someone I rarely talk to? Or someone I don't talk to about my actual joys and struggles?*

There is something about a face-to-face interaction with my friend (and in the same room if at all possible—video chat isn't nearly as good) that uniquely allows me to enter into his life, ask wise questions, explore secret areas of struggle, and laugh over life's ups and downs. We need to live with a mindset that resists substituting technology for friendship or chitchat for conversation. Because the truth is we cannot hack human nature—we cannot escape from the way God made us. If we truly want biblical friendship, there is simply no substitute for good old-fashioned conversation.

Shared Meals: Please Pass the Joy

Among all the shared activities that can help build biblical friendship through conversation, meals offer a special yet often-neglected opportunity. I don't mean just eating at the same table. I mean *sharing meals together*: there's a difference. When you share a meal, you're not simply filling your fuel tank and then running off to do something you consider more important. Sharing meals is not about efficiency, and it certainly isn't about multitasking. It's about engaging with one another in one of the richest expressions of humanity.

In his book *A Meal With Jesus*, Tim Chester records a 33 percent decrease in families eating together over the last 30 years and a 45 percent decrease in friends doing so.[37]

He comments, "Meals slow things down. Some of us don't like that. We like to get things done. But meals force you to be people oriented instead of task oriented. Sharing a meal is not the only way to build relationships, but it is number one on the list."[38]

Whether or not you agree with Chester that meals are number one on that particular list, we all know that a shared meal can create a special opportunity for thoughtful, face-to-face conversation. Meals have provided my wife and me wonderful opportunities for forging friendships. As just one example, what began as my personal search for a spiritual mentor gradually developed into a wonderful tradition of us sharing Sunday-evening meals with an older couple who have become genuine friends. Welcoming them into our home has enabled us to welcome them into our lives, and they have enriched our walks with Christ, both as individuals and as a couple. The simple practice of truly sharing meals together set the stage for a beautiful biblical friendship.

Caring Confrontation: Beyond Happy Talk

In the course of building a biblical friendship, many conversations can and should be simple, easy, and enjoyable. But if we're serious about having a friendship that exists to increasingly glorify God, then at times our talk will have to venture into less comfortable territory. This is when the topic of our sanctification, that lifelong process of putting off sinful habits and practices and putting on greater Christlikeness, comes to the forefront. Sanctification involves those areas in our lives we would prefer not to talk about—areas of weakness and vulnerability and persistent sin patterns. Yet biblical friendship calls us to go where our sin nature fears to tread.

It helps to view the discomfort of these deeper conversations as sacrifices—something we wouldn't naturally want to do but are willing or even glad to do for the sake of another. Jesus' words in John 15:13 draw a perfectly clear connection between friendship and personal sacrifice: "Greater love has no one than this, that someone lay down his life for his friends." If self-sacrifice and service were the ultimate ways in which Jesus showed his friendship and love for us, then we must expect a measure of sacrifice to be essential—not optional—to the development of biblical friendships.

By God's grace, we can allow the indwelling Spirit to draw us forward into this more difficult conversational territory. We can take on a Christ-like attitude of sacrificial service for the same basic reasons Jesus laid down his life for us—for God's glory, Christ's kingdom, and the good of others.

Here are some practical kickstarter questions, best asked thoughtfully and graciously.

How can I pray for you?
Where are you struggling?
Where have you experienced God's grace in your struggle?
Where has God been up to good in your life recently?
What is bringing joy to your heart?
Where do you see me growing spiritually?
How can I be a better friend to you?

Biblical friendship is forged through willing sacrifice, a desire to go beyond a habit of happy talk into a culture of caring confrontation, a place where sanctification can flourish. Putting our personal comfort on the altar in this way beautifully follows Jesus' example of love and pursuit.

This aspect of biblical friendship was mostly absent from my life up through high school. When I got to college, however, much of that changed. This was both painful and very positive.

I remember one particular meeting I had with the resident director who oversaw my area of ministry. When he asked how I was doing, I replied how busy I was. That may seem like an innocent answer, but for me, appealing to my schedule had become a blanket excuse that I imagined justified all the sinful habits I had developed— my distance, my impatience, my lack of love, my lack of consideration, and more. Sure, I was busy, and busy doing some good things, but I had taken the easy path of letting my busyness build a wall between myself and others. In a very short time I had become the classic isolated leader, someone so busy serving that he never seemed to have time to let anyone into his life. In replying, "I'm busy," I thought I could avoid a deeper conversation…after all, we can't let the meeting run over schedule, can we?

I'm sure my friend had seen this happen with zealous young men before, and even though it was likely to draw the conversation into uncomfortable territory, he knew me well enough to say exactly the right thing.

"Jonathan, maybe you're too busy."

Up until then, my "busy, busy" line had worked

like a charm. People nodded their heads, in sympathy or empathy, and I walked away with a renewed rationalization for my wayward course. But somehow this simple sentence pulled me up short. The well-deserved sense of guilt that had been lingering in my conscience rose up, driving me in the direction of repentance. I began to see how easily I could get wrapped into my own agenda at the expense of other people. I had come to equate busyness with godliness, and to prefer doing things *for* people over being *with* people. That one sentence wasn't the end of our conversation, but as the Spirit of God used my friend's willingness to step out of the comfort zone, it was the perfect beginning.

So yes, there are things you can and should do to foster the development of biblical friendships.

- Invest time in developing friendships.
- Embrace the right attitudes and goals.
- Utilize shared activities to build relationships on a number of levels, but ultimately to create contexts for redemptive, sanctifying conversation.

All of these, when done in the Spirit's enabling power, help produce truly Christ-centered (and therefore biblical) friendships. It will take time to make meaningful progress, but consistency can yield a fruitful relationship—a fragrant reminder of God's grace in this life.

To talk and laugh and do kindness to each other; to read pleasant books together; to make jokes together and then talk seriously together; to be sometimes teaching and sometimes learning…These and other similar expressions of feeling, which proceed from the hearts of those who love and are loved in return, and are revealed in the face, the voice, the eyes, and in a thousand charming ways, were like a kindling fire to melt our souls together and out of many to make us one.[39]

Dig Deeper

1. Think through some of your closest spiritual friendships. How did they form? How did they grow?
2. What do you find most difficult in forging new friendships and cultivating existing friendships?
3. Think through where God has placed you. Where are there natural opportunities for you to share life together with a friend?
4. List out 2-3 people you would like to pursue, and a goal for each to help you begin.

Five

THREATS TO BIBLICAL FRIENDSHIP

Forewarned is Forearmed

Our brief journey toward a better understanding of biblical friendship has taken us down some paths that I hope you've found helpful. Let's take a moment to review what we have learned so far.

In the first chapter we gained a rudimentary grasp of the origin, nature, and challenges of biblical friendship, ending with a working definition. Next, we uncovered the leading friendship substitutes and saw why they are, by comparison, so weak and inadequate. In chapter three, we identified four of the outstanding attributes of biblical friendship as revealed in Scripture, so we know how to recognize the real thing. And in chapter four we learned about the key attitudes, goals, and techniques we can and should use in order to cooperate with God in the forming and forging of biblical friendships.

At every step, there's been a consistent theme—as

a rule, biblical friendship doesn't come easily, and any friendships we do form in this fallen world will face frequent and varied opposition. I hope you're not surprised by this. Jesus promised that following him was not going to be the easy way in this life. The best way? Yes. The most rewarding way, both now and especially hereafter? Absolutely. But the easiest way? No.

Therefore, it's vital that we devote a chapter to exploring threats to biblical friendship. I've selected four areas that we especially need to be aware of and understand.

- Personal sin
- An incomplete grasp of the gospel
- False expectations
- The homophobia bogeyman

Personal Sin

We have already seen how the world, the flesh, and the devil are continually opposed to friendships that seek to reflect the relationships of the Trinity. While this opposition can take many forms, the goal is always the same: to tempt us into sinning against God and one another. Pastor Rusty McKie broadens the scope with this thought:

> Friendships matter because through them you image God to a broken world, displaying the good news of the gospel which is a message of reconciliation (2 Corinthians 5:18–20). This is why the Dark Trinity [our flesh, the world, Satan] hates friendships so much. Destroy the image; destroy the message. As

much as we are caught up in this cosmic drama, thankfully we don't have to fight alone.[40]

Indeed, thank God we do not have to fight this battle for biblical friendship alone; the Word of God and the indwelling Holy Spirit offer us everything we need to be victorious.

It's no accident that Paul discusses spiritual warfare immediately after giving instruction about three crucial kinds of relationships: husband-wife, parents-children, and employer-employee. In reading Ephesians 5 and 6 as a unit, you can almost see Paul's thought process as he moves seamlessly from the challenges of relationships to the need to battle against Satan's spiritual attacks. It may seem to us that our interpersonal conflicts operate exclusively on the human level, but Paul is telling us they do not. "For *we do not wrestle against flesh and blood*, but against the rulers, against the authorities, against the cosmic powers over this present darkness, against the spiritual forces of evil in the heavenly places" (Ephesians 6:12).

In other words, when it comes to interpersonal conflict, you are never my enemy, and I am never yours, regardless of how either of us may feel in the midst of the disagreement. The "wrestling" we experience is not against flesh and blood. Our real enemy is a big, mixed-up tumbleweed of spiritual forces that tempt us to *act* sinfully or adopt sinful *attitudes* toward one another.

Like all temptations, these emanate from this fallen world, Satan's forces, and our own sin nature. Satan is rabidly focused on undermining our redemptive relation-ships, especially those that bear a gospel witness. The more explicitly biblical a friendship, therefore, the greater we can expect the opposition to be. Because Satan will spare no effort to mar or destroy the image and witness of God, believers must guard against spiritual threats to biblical friendship.

Once again, these explicitly spiritual attacks appear in a form we may not think of as spiritual, and this itself is part of Satan's deception. They appear as everyday, run-of-the-mill *temptations to sin against one another*, "wrestl[ing] against flesh and blood." Yet interpersonal conflict is profoundly spiritual—every bit as spiritual as reading the Bible, singing to the Lord, or listening to preaching. Indeed, how we respond to such temptations represents the front-line, hand-to-hand combat of the spiritual life. These are some of the moments that matter most. They are spirituality applied to real life.

It is no surprise that the Proverbs, which speak so highly of friendship's value, should also warn against what tears friendships apart. The Proverbs identify four threats to your friendship: hurtful speech (essentially gossip and slander), dishonest speech, anger, and jealousy.

Hurtful Speech

A whisperer separates close friends (Proverbs 16:28b)

Whoever goes about slandering reveals secrets, but he who is trustworthy in spirit keeps a thing covered (Proverbs 11:13).

With his mouth the godless man would destroy his neighbor (Proverbs 11:9a).

Gossip and slander undermine the very things essential to any relationship: trust, love, fidelity, and interpersonal rapport. When one friend speaks about another in a hurtful way, the results can be devastating. "A brother [or sister] offended is more unyielding than a strong city" (Proverbs 18:19a). James has something similar in mind when, in discussing the dangers of unwise speech, he writes "How great a forest is set ablaze by such a small fire!" (James 3:5). So even though gossip and slander can (and should) be forgiven like any other sin, it can take a considerable time for trust to be rebuilt, and the hard truth is that many friendships never recover fully. As Blaise Pascal writes in his *Pensées*, "I set this down as a fact, that if all men knew what each said of the other, there would not be four friends in the world."[41] Pascal's humor only highlights the reality that hurtful speech is a principal destroyer of friendship.

I vividly remember a particular chain of gossip I was involved in during college. I had guiltily passed along to one friend a bit of gossip about a second friend. A few days later, I was the object of a related piece of gossip (ever notice how sin produces sin?), and I was indignant. Even though the gossip hurt me, somehow I didn't see my own gossiping as equally sinful and hurtful to another. As a third friend pointed out (bluntly but helpfully), I had inserted myself into the midst of other people's business and shouldn't have been surprised that I ended up getting burned.

To this day, I remain grateful for that reminder of my sinful tendencies, and of the fact that hurtful words have no place in biblical friendships.

Dishonest Speech

A dishonest man spreads strife (Proverbs 16:28a)

Do not deceive with your lips (Proverbs 24:28b)

A lying tongue hates its victims (Proverbs 26:28)

Whereas gossip works behind the scenes in friendship, dishonest speech happens face-to-face. Why do we end up lying to each other? Often it's because, as sinners, we love our own comfort and prize our autonomy — and aren't our friends the ones most likely to get in the way of those selfish desires?

Most of us probably don't think we're dishonest with our friends in this way, but consider…How about telling your friend you will pray for him or her or offering some kind of practical assistance, and then not following through or even following up? How about declining or canceling an opportunity to get together by passing off a minor reason as the core reason? Our dishonesty can easily tempt others to be offended, even when we're not blatantly trying to mislead or "get away with" something. Dishonesty is fertile soil for misunderstanding and offense. It thrives in the small, dark corners of our half-truths.

Another form of dishonesty we do not often consider is flattery. Proverbs 29:5 and 28:23 read, "A man who flatters his neighbor spreads a net for his feet.…

Whoever rebukes a man will afterward find more favor than he who flatters with his tongue." And Proverbs 26:28 draws a straight line between lying and flattery, "A lying tongue hates its victims, and a flattering mouth works ruin."

Flattery is the "positive" form of dishonesty. Not to be confused with encouragement, flattery drips praise but issues from an ill motive. Hugh Black writes, "The flatterer will take good care not to offend our susceptibilities by too many shocks of wholesome truth-telling."[42] Flattery in friendship finds its roots in people-pleasing and fear of man. When I reject the Bible's counsel to speak truth in love, I will turn to flattery to try to maintain an appearance of friendship. Flattery is all form and no substance. According to Proverbs, when I make a show of genuine friendship through flattery, I may seem to be building up the other person, but all I'm doing is setting him up for disappointment, ruin, and entrapment.

Anger

A hot-tempered man stirs up strife, but he who is slow to anger quiets contention (Proverbs 15:18)

Make no friendship with a man given to anger, nor go with a wrathful man, lest you learn his ways and entangle yourself in a snare (Proverbs 22:24–25)

Anger emerges from unmet expectations. If you don't give me something I want (respect, attention, honesty, love, time, or a thousand other possibilities), my sin nature will always be tempted to respond with anger. But don't think anger is limited to red-in-the-face, clenched-fist, barely-controlled rage. That's just one point on a broad spectrum. Less obvious signs of anger include coldness, isolation, pouting, withdrawal, sulking, sarcasm, malice, cynicism, irritation, and plain old frustration.

Perhaps you see a photo on Facebook of friends at a gathering and wonder why you were not invited. Instead of overlooking the issue or asking your friend, you allow the imagined offense to stew in your heart. Hang onto that offense, and it will inevitably affect your attitude toward the person or people involved. From there it will affect your speech and interactions. Your next meeting will be less warm and gracious, and tinged with doubt and suspicion. The friendship is now suffering because you have made assumptions (probably sinful, self-righteous ones) that may have no basis in reality.

The Bible is helpful and clarifying here, urging us to be *slow to anger* (James 1:19). When an unmet expectation tempts you to anger, ask God for the grace to not simply react. Instead, seek to redeem that situation by recognizing it as an opportunity to overlook in love, believe the best about your friend(s), speak the truth in love, or pray fervently for them. Or maybe all four.

Jealousy

> *For jealousy makes a man furious, and he will not spare when he takes revenge* (Proverbs 6:34).

> *Wrath is cruel, anger is overwhelming, but who can stand before jealousy?* (Proverbs 27:4).

Where anger involves expectations, jealousy involves aspirations. So while jealousy and anger often arise together, jealousy is worth looking at separately. Jealousy emerges from a different heart motivation and often produces different problems in a friendship.

Because jealousy involves aspirations, it can present itself as a somewhat respectable sin. After all, it is good and godly to aspire to greater things for the glory of God in response to his leading. Yet godly aspiration can quickly be warped and corrupted by jealousy when we begin to turn our attention to those whom we perceive to have more in some area than we do. Jealousy kicks in when we start to focus, not on what God has called us to do or be, but on a perceived gap between ourselves and others. At that point, our attention has shifted from obeying God to idolizing what we think someone else possesses. This can be almost anything—physical or spiritual gifts, material possessions, attainments, relationships, etc. It doesn't matter if they actually have (for example) a better marriage, or actually derive satisfaction from (for example) a cooler car. Jealousy grows out of our belief that what someone else has or seems to have would make us happy.

Jealousy turns us away from God's good gifts—what he has given us, why he has done so, and how we can develop these gifts further. It tempts us to reject God's purpose and path for our life in favor of our own path. Our spiritual and practical pursuits for God's glory ought to be characterized by joy, gratitude, and perseverance. But when jealousy controls our hearts, joy can be crowded out by bitterness, gratitude by anger, and perseverance by grasping. Once we start to focus on what is missing in our lives, jealousy tempts us to begin manipulating people and circumstances in order to get what we want. Clearly, persistent jealousy and biblical friendship cannot coexist.

One of my first jobs put me into close proximity with a dynamic and charismatic personality. We developed a good working relationship and friendship, but after a few months I began to notice changes in my heart toward this man. He was funny, gregarious, outgoing, charming, and had a way of putting people at ease—all traits that are typically in short supply for me. As a rule, people warm to him quickly and become more drawn to him over time. I realized I was becoming jealous of his gifts and talents.

As we continued working together and our friendship grew, this nagging sense of jealousy grew alongside it, eventually eroding my focus on Christ. I doubt this man even knew I was struggling, but I was increasingly aware that my jealousy was keeping me from loving God wisely and pursuing him wholeheartedly. Instead my interactions with this man became marked by hypocrisy and bitterness. By God's grace God, I finally saw that the only person this was harming was me. Then, instead of focusing on the perceived deficits and weaknesses I believed my friend's strengths exposed in me, I was able to be thankful for the unique way God had equipped and blessed my friend *and* me.

An Incomplete Grasp of the Gospel

Biblical friendship between two Christians requires them to practice an unusual level of transparency. But the very prospect of having to be that open can lead many of us to conclude that we don't even want to try. The reason for this reluctance is simple: we fear the repercussions if we are actually honest about our struggles. We don't want to be isolated, shunned, or seen as second-class believers.

These kinds of fears flow necessarily from an inadequate understanding of the gospel.

Through his sinless life, his finished work on the cross, and his victorious resurrection, Jesus has purchased our salvation and satisfied God's righteous wrath toward all our sin—past, present, and future. He has given us a new heart and placed his Spirit within us and is daily changing us more and more into his image. We are indeed new creations and by virtue of this are destined for an eternity of sinless perfection.

But who are we right now?

The biblical answer is that, even as we are adopted children of God and counted righteous in his sight, *at the same time we are—every single one of us—frail creatures who struggle with specific sins that are tied to our areas of personal weakness.* An inadequate grasp of the gospel fails to take sufficient account of the second part of that sentence. This tends to turn the Christian life into a purity contest, an exercise in pretense. Faith, hope, and love become polluted by denial, fear, and mistrust.

What shall we do about the fact that we still struggle with particular areas of sin? Hide it and pretend we are better than we really are? Or admit it and enlist selected others to help us in our daily challenge?

People intent on portraying a false image never let

their guard down long enough to allow others inside. We often do this is because our churches have a culture that classifies struggling Christians as inferior and undesirable. But the truth is we all struggle. We all have parts of our character that are inferior and undesirable. And we will never have biblical friends unless we allow those inferior and undesirable parts of our character to become known to our closest friends.

The gospel is not only the most wonderful truth of all. It is the deepest and most multilayered truth, the one we will be celebrating for eternity. If you want to have biblical friendship, study the gospel until you realize we are all weak and needy. Then you will be willing to admit your own flaws to others, and you won't be shocked when you find out the extent to which weakness and neediness characterize even the greatest believers you know.

False Expectations

Given all the areas of Jesus' life on which the Bible is silent, isn't it fascinating that we have so much information about his friendships? Clearly he had an attractive personality, and during his public ministry he socialized actively with a broad range of people. But through it all we see two constants: there were twelve with whom he spent most of his time, and just three with whom he was especially close.

In his humanity, Jesus had limitations on his time and "psychological bandwidth," just like you and I do. God chose to show us in his Word that even the divine Son could only maintain a limited number of what we are calling biblical friendships. The reminder here for us is that biblical friendship takes place entirely within the context of finite human nature. So, even though God can individually stretch us and our abilities, we all reach a limit on our capacity for such friendship. Being aware of this can prevent us from developing a couple of common false expectations.

- First, we shouldn't expect to have a substantial number of close biblical friendships.
- Second, we shouldn't expect to develop a biblical friendship with a particular person just because we want to.

Based on what I have experienced and observed, biblical friendships do not emerge from striving or grasping. They emerge from a gospel-motivated willingness to serve and love others and a trust that God will gradually guide us into biblical friendships as we follow his leading. Sometimes these friendships end up being with "shared interest" people whom we easily gravitate toward. At other times, we may be surprised at the good work God does in our lives through unlikely friendships.

Catching a vision for the depth and beauty of biblical friendship can be emotionally challenging for some. If we expect our friendships to exceed what is depicted in Scripture, we are setting ourselves up for disappointment, sorrow, and failure, thus opening the door to bitterness and misunderstanding. But if we remember that everyone has limited capacity for friendship and seek to keep our hearts grounded in the truth that God's plans—including his plans for friendship—are the best possible thing for us, we can avoid false expectations as we pray for and seek out biblical friendship.

The reality that everyone possesses a limited "friendship bandwidth" also has implications for local church dynamics. As a pastor, I find that people desire close friendships with their church leaders, and this is a very good thing. But no one can maintain a large number of biblical friendships while also maintaining their quality. The pastor who displays a spirit of Christian love toward church members—while maintaining actual biblical friendships with a relative few—probably isn't engaged in hypocrisy or false sentiment. Most likely he's just doing the best he can with the time and capacity God has granted.

Church leaders are just human beings trying to communicate something of the perfect love of God to people with whom they will, as a practical matter, never be able to form a close personal bond. Give your leaders the grace to occupy that difficult role, and enjoy the spirit of Christian fellowship it engenders.

The Homophobia Bogeyman

In recent years, the Western world has undergone a revolution in the visibility and acceptance of a surprisingly broad range of alternative expressions of sexuality. To the extent your worldview has been formed by popular culture, you will be under the impression that same-sex attraction, for example, is not only perfectly normal but quite common. As a result, you may think you're seeing signs of it everywhere.

In the midst of this cultural confusion regarding

human sexuality, I believe the testimony of Scripture is clear that homosexuality was not part of God's original intent and design. I believe homosexuality is sinful, and one of many signs of a broken world, fractured relationships, and disordered sexuality. However, in saying this, I am not sure the church has moved further than simply identifying the problem.

Within the church, spiritual friendship as a discipline is under-utilized as a way of addressing this culturally sensitive topic. Many believers are afraid of any close same-sex friendship, especially with someone who struggles with same-sex attraction. Such hypervigilance has had serious implications for the formation of healthy, everyday same-sex friendships. The challenges may be greater for men than for women—since it's more socially acceptable for women to show affection for one another—but this dynamic affects us all. These challenges can appear in two basic ways.

- Concern for appearances: *What if people think my same-sex friend and I are in or heading toward a sexual relationship?*
- Concern for honesty and integrity: *What if my same-sex friend struggles (or what if I struggle) with* same-sex attraction *and our friendship becomes a source of temptation?*

Concern for Appearances

C.S. Lewis addresses this notion head-on in *The Four Loves*, writing "This imposes on me at the outset a very tiresome bit of demolition. It has actually become necessary in our time to rebut the theory that every firm and serious friendship is really homosexual."[43]

That sort of demolition is in order. If you think intellectuals were imagining homosexuals in every closet when Lewis wrote those words in the late 1950s, today the matter has reached absurd proportions. Several articles appearing around the release of the third *Lord of the Rings* movie reveled in supposed homoerotic overtones in the relationship between Frodo and Sam. Similar comments have been made about the friendship between David and Jonathan. Western society has become on the one hand so hyper-sexualized and on the other so typified by isolation and alienation that many of us can no longer comprehend even the possibility of a deep and meaningful same-sex friendship that is devoid of a sexual component.

This is a tragedy. Such an absurd perspective cheapens and warps the biblical ideal of friendship and can even cripple it among those who should know better. Indeed, I know several Christians, males and females, who find this level of intimacy in friendship frightening, entirely on the basis of what others might think.

As Christians, we are called to stand up for biblical truth in whatever era and society we may live. In our day and age, part of what it means to be a believer is to let our lives and words testify that same-sex friendships can be deep and rewarding—complete with kindness, genuine affection, and a comforting spirit—without anything even vaguely approaching homoeroticism.

Concern for Honesty and Integrity

At the same time, same-sex attraction is obviously an issue for some people. It would be wrong, therefore, for me to tell you that concern for sexual integrity in a same-sex friendship is a complete non-issue. A few guidelines may therefore be helpful.

If you struggle with same-sex attraction, then the more your friendship is grounded in the gospel, the more likely it will be for your struggle to come up in conversation, and the more comfortable you should feel in getting it out in the open. Try to do this fairly early in the friendship as a matter of honesty and integrity with your friend, and so you can enlist him or her to help you in prayer and perhaps counsel.

In the same way, if you have any real concern about the possibility of same-sex attraction in someone with whom you are building a biblical friendship, see if you can't take the initiative to bring up the subject in a way that is kind and invites open and honest conversation.[44]

In either case, as a matter of caution, wisdom, and accountability, the two of you should agree to make a trusted third person aware that you are trying to build a godly relationship and at least one of you struggles with homosexual tendencies.

I know for most of us these will be difficult conversations. However, as we discussed in the previous chapter, we are called to emulate our Savior by sacrificing our ease and comfort for the good of others. In fact, within the bounds of Christian friendship, there can be great opportunity to display Christian love and friendship to those who struggle with same-sex attraction.

Wesley Hill, a prominent writer on this topic, adds a helpful perspective:[45]

> Gay and lesbian Christians who, by virtue of
> their biblical and traditional convictions, commit
> themselves to a life of celibacy may find that they
> are thereby positioned to befriend others and to
> be befriended. Far from being asked to deny their
> impulse to reach out for communion and compan-
> ionship, they may find that impulse sanctified, taken
> up, and transmuted in a divine economy that is
> always in the business of dispensing grace in the midst
> of (not only in the removal of) human weakness.[46]

Do not miss the significance of what Hill writes. Christians who struggle with same-sex attraction need to be be*friended* in the bonds of Christian friendship, precisely for our *mutual* sanctification. To befriend someone who struggles in this way gives us a vital oppor-tunity to show the love of Christ powerfully.[47]

So, having reviewed these various threats to biblical friendship, let us be reminded that any relationship seeking to glorify God will come under attack. Instead of allowing the world, Satan, and our flesh to tear apart and break down our friendships, however, let us instead learn to walk in the grace of our Lord and Savior Jesus Christ. If not for the grace of God in our lives, we quickly revert back to old practices that threaten the development of God-glorifying friendships. Each day let us earnestly seek God's grace and mercy to walk in a manner worthy of the calling we have received, and then to show that grace and mercy to our friends.

In our final chapter, we will see the good that true, Christ-centered friendships can bring into our lives. The fruits of biblical friendship should not be the primary motivation in seeking friends, but are nonetheless sweet graces from our Savior as we walk along this journey together.

Dig Deeper

1. Consider the four sins described in this chapter— hurtful speech, dishonest speech, anger, jealousy. Are there friendships where you need to seek forgiveness and reconciliation?

2. List out some expectations you have of your friend- ships. Should any of them be re-evaluated in light of what you've learned so far?

3. Does the "homophobia bogeyman" keep you from developing the type of friendships elaborated on in this book?

Six

THE PURPOSE OF BIBLICAL FRIENDSHIP

Cultivating and Displaying Unity

In Aelred of Rievaulx's, *Spiritual Friendship*, Aelred's friend Walter asks an honest question and, in the process, makes an important point.

> Since, therefore, I have read this excellent discussion on the nature of friendship, I should like to have you tell me what practical advantages it procures for those who cultivate it…[It] is only when its purpose and benefit are understood that it will be sought after with genuine ardor.[48]

Perhaps you have a question similar to Walter's. *Are biblical friendships really worth the effort? What are they meant to accomplish, and what changes do they bring?* In this closing chapter, I want you to catch a vision for the vital role biblical friendship plays—not merely in wonderfully enhancing our individual lives, but more importantly as an essential instrument in the accomplishment of God's purposes.

A Picture Worth a Thousand Words

The gospel, as we have seen, must be communicated person-to-person through words. The various fruits of the gospel, including biblical friendships, can likewise be described. But since these words about the gospel and its fruits so often emphasize changed lives, what really matters is whether lives have actually been changed! Thus, nothing proves the gospel better interpersonally than when the fruit of the gospel is evident.

Biblical friendship, in particular, is a fruit of the gospel that uniquely witnesses to a reality greater than this life and its daily challenges. More than any other relationship, biblical friendship demonstrates to the world a spiritual unity rooted in the supernatural.[49]

In John 17, Jesus speaks of those roots. In the midst of the rich theology suffused through Jesus' high priestly prayer to his Father, we get a glimpse of an amazing truth: believers in unity with one another mirror the unity of the Trinity, and that unity serves as a divine witness. Listen to Jesus' words,

> I do not ask for these only [his disciples], but also
> for those who will believe in me through their word,
> that they may all be one, just as you, Father, are in me,
> and I in you, that they also may be in us, so that the

world may believe that you have sent me. The glory that you have given me I have given to them, that they may be one even as we are one, I in them and you in me, that they may become perfectly one, so that the world may know that you sent me and loved them even as you loved me (John 17:20–23).

Take careful note here: the unity that Jesus prays for us to enjoy is not achieved through our feeble attempts at similarity and solidarity. It is not a product of human agreement and alliance. Our unity is a reflected unity, an image of the Trinity's perfect and eternal unity. And our unity is a redeemed unity, a unity granted to us through Jesus' atoning work on the cross, by which he brought sinners like you and me into his family. This oneness of the Trinity that we glimpse in Jesus' prayer—"just as you, Father, are in me, and I in you"—becomes a permanent part of the individual identity of each one of us.

I must say it again…this unity among believers is not achieved *by us*; it is *established for us* through the person and work of Jesus Christ. Flowing out of the supernatural reality of our pre-existing unity in Christ, our unity with other believers is *experienced* as we pursue biblical friendship. Through biblical friendship we can increasingly understand, experience, cultivate, and display the supernatural unity that Christ died to give us through our justification and redemption. Biblical friendship makes us more aware of and more fulfilled by that which is already true.

Thus, biblical friendships carry within them

something greater and more awesome than you may have ever imagined. By demonstrating unity in a world characterized by division, they tell the story of the gospel in a way nothing else can.

Persistence by Grace, not Perfection by Effort

Like every other aspect of our maturation in Christ, this pursuit of experiential unity among believers through biblical friendship is always a work in progress because the world, the flesh, and the devil will never cease their opposition. Jesus therefore prays that this new community of people he has redeemed out of the world would display unity. He prays, "I in them and you in me, that they may become perfectly one."

That perfect unity *will* be fully experienced in the next life. For now, however, we're continually working toward it as it gets fleshed out gradually. This process, with all its challenges and messiness, speaks of a gospel that corresponds to the reality of this fallen world, while at the same time offering so much more.

Even as Christians, we often have to remind ourselves that the gospel isn't a magic wand that makes our problems vanish with a twinkle. The gospel breaks into this fallen world, and for those who are saved by it, it permanently and radically changes our eternal future. It also profoundly alters the present. But it does not take us out of the world or insulate us from its troubles, challenges, and temptations (see what Jesus says in this same high-priestly prayer, in verse 15). God leaves us in the midst of this fallen world for the sake of others, that we might shine the light of the gospel to the glory of his name. Each of us is called to shine that light in a particular way depending on our giftings and callings (dentist, student, pastor, homemaker, etc.). But all of us are called to shine that light in the context of our interpersonal relationships, especially with other believers.

In order to bear witness to the truth of the gospel, therefore, biblical friendships don't have to be perfect. They just have to prove themselves genuine by enduring through the ups and downs, the successes and failures.

In the life of an individual Christian, one-off victories over temptation and sin are certainly important, but no one of them is ultimate. What matters is the long game— it's a marathon, not a sprint. Our faith is ultimately proved genuine as we endure, by grace, to the end. If our individual walks with the Lord are so characterized by instability, imperfection, and weakness, why should we imagine that biblical friendships must somehow be seamless and perfect to be legitimate?

The gospel offers everlasting hope and tangible spiritual change that is nevertheless realistic and true to the challenge of living in a world so obviously fallen. With beautiful, brutal honesty, biblical friendships can testify to the world of that life-changing, hope-giving gospel.

Cultivating and Displaying Unity

Biblical friendships can therefore be a witness in two ways. They can bear testimony, primarily within the church, to the unity of the body of Christ and the wonderful ways in which that unity can be experienced and expressed. And they can bear witness to the power of the gospel before a lost and dying world desperate for real and meaningful relationships with God and others.

Within the Body of Christ

Publicly living out biblical friendship within the context of the local church is largely an act of mutual encouragement in the faith. An entire book could be written on this subject alone. But for now I'll just focus on three aspects. Each one is, at the same time, a fruit of biblical friendship and way of pursuing it further.

<u>**Redeeming ordinary moments.**</u> One of my mentors from college, now a close friend, would always drill into me, "Never do anything alone." While he obviously didn't mean this literally, the principle is sound (and the overstatement made it memorable).

By "redeeming ordinary moments," I simply mean that some of the regular activities of daily life can be enhanced as we do them with others. Everyday life can be experienced on a different level when shared in the context of biblical friendship. Common interests can here become an enhancement rather than a hindrance to biblical friendship. "The idea seems so simple," write Jay Pathak and Dave Runyon, "just do what you're already doing, invite others to the table, and watch what God does as a result."[50]

If we consign friendship to just one sphere of life such as church, work, or hobbies, the very idea of friendship tends to become compartmentalized and utilitarian. But if our friendship is centered on "life together" (Bonhoeffer's classic phrase), then the redemption of ordinary moments becomes a natural impulse.

Depending on how your life is structured, there may not be many opportunities for you to redeem the ordinary moments in this way. But consider John 17, how the cultivation and display of Christian unity is so vital to God's plan. Could you possibly reorder certain aspects of your life to make room for more and better biblical friendships?

There is great benefit to be had here if we will choose to live a little differently. To make that choice is to adopt a God-glorifying mindset that presses our hearts in the direction of actually wanting, as much as possible, to live daily life together with other believers.

Practicing informal counseling. When a group of people truly understand the purpose and value of biblical friendship, and begin spending time with one another in real-life situations, informal counseling can begin to take place so naturally they may not even realize it's happening. [51] Even if your church has a formalized counseling ministry, imagine how the congregation could benefit from biblical relationships that make informal counseling a natural, comfortable practice. When friends are sharing burdens, walking through suffering together, and encouraging and affirming one another, the body of Christ is stronger. When friends are confronting and caring for one another and calling one another to personal holiness, the body of Christ is healthier. Biblical friendship cultivated and displayed within a local church is self-replicating—it encourages more of the same as people come to recognize that you don't need to be among the "spiritual elite" to enjoy its benefits.

Experiencing embedded accountability. You may be familiar with the concept of the "embedded journalist," a kind of reporter sometimes active in wartime. These journalists are not the kind who show up one day, interview a few people, and return to their safe haven. Embedded journalists live among and travel with troops in a war. They are woven into the fabric of the story they're trying to cover. This is the idea I'm getting at in the phrase "embedded accountability."

If you've been active in a local church, you probably know how easily traditional accountability can flounder. For example, a young man struggling with pornography is paired to an older, wiser man for accountability. For the first few weeks the older of the pair asks the younger if he has struggled. "Have you looked at anything you shouldn't have? Have you been pure?" Their conversations are typically awkward, vague, and unfruitful. Before too long, these men are avoiding each other at church meetings and their "accountability relationship" is soon forgotten. Why? The accountability wasn't embedded in a biblical friendship. The motivations were good and godly, but *wanting* to practice accountability isn't enough. Accountability relationships ultimately succeed or fail on the quality of the relationship itself.

I don't know if this is universally true, but it has certainly been true in my own experience as a pastor and biblical counselor—*accountability that is not embedded into a pre-existing biblical relationship never works*. That's right, never. I say this simply because every single time I have seen accountability flourish it has been part of a biblical friendship.

That speaks loudly to me. It tells me that one of the most wonderful fruits and one of the most fruitful purposes of biblical friendship is that it makes embedded accountability possible. Grounded in Christ and his gospel, biblical friendship allows accountability to become as natural and normal a topic of conversation as any other shared interest.

All three of these opportunities—redemption of ordinary moments, informal counseling, and embedded accountability—help the church live out our shared union in Christ.

Before a Watching World

Biblical friendships lived out *in* the church witness *to* the church in one way. But biblical friendships lived out in the world witness to the world in quite a different way. Perhaps you've seen something like this at the level of servanthood.

A family in a local church needs to move to a new home. Word goes out within the church that on moving day they could use some help loading and unloading the rental truck (donuts and/or pizza could be involved). When that day comes, the people in the new neighborhood are treated to an unusual spectacle. *How big is the family moving into this house? Who are all these people unloading the truck?* When the neighbors learn that these helpers are not family members, and not neighbors from their old community, but just friends from church, that gets noticed. That says something unusual.

If simple acts of servanthood to one another can begin to speak a gospel witness to the world, how much more a lived pattern of biblical friendship that endures over time? We find the roots of this once again in Jesus' high priestly prayer. There in John 17, we see that unity among believers, which finds its origin and pattern within the Trinity, serves an even greater purpose: "that the world may know that you sent me and loved them even as you loved me."

Dick Lucas explains it well, writing "the purpose of this unity is evangelistic. Jesus' desire is that the world should see his people's unity in the truth as it is worked out in relationships within the church, and that people in the world would, on account of this, come to believe the message for themselves."[52]

We must resist our natural, fallen tendency to live our lives in isolated, impenetrable fortresses of self-focus and fear. This compromises the message of the unifying gospel we are called to share. If Jesus' earthly mission was to make the Father known to the world and to redeem a people for his Father, then biblical friendship is a necessary and essential means by which we carry on in that same pursuit. You, and Christians in your local church, can offer a living example of divinely empowered biblical friendship to a curious, perplexed, and desperate world.

Until We See His Glory

As I reflect on this topic of friendship, I find myself echoing Ralph Waldo Emerson's words, "I awoke this morning with devout thanksgiving for my friends, the old and the new. Shall I not call God the Beautiful, who daily showeth himself so to me in his gifts?"[53]

God, in his mercy, gives us friends as gifts and graces for life's journey. For most of my life I have been the recipient of friendships that have demonstrated God's love to me in marvelous ways. Earlier in this book I alluded to the fact that my adolescent years were particularly lonely, a loneliness I tried to mask through artificial extroversion and overcompensation. While I wanted real and authentic friendships, I didn't understand what friendship was truly about. Yet even in that difficult season God provided two very special friendships that helped me live out my faith. Today, both those friendships remain an integral part of my walk with Christ.

When I went off to college, away from the nest of family and familiarity, my friendships took on new dimensions, becoming much more a part of daily life. Many of these friendships, instead of being founded on common interests and hobbies, emerged directly from a shared faith in Christ. One of these friends, Nathan, loves soccer and basketball, hunting and fishing. I couldn't connect with him on any of those, yet our friendship flourished. Nathan models vulnerability and transparency, and is always ready to move the conversation from the mundane to the meaningful.

My friend Joe has a personality characterized by

compassion, laughter, and humor — vital counterpoints to my often serious and introverted nature. What began as a mentor/discipler relationship has evolved wonderfully into a friendship of mutual encouragement and accountability.

My friendship with Scott actually grew out of a confrontation. But from a simple conversation over lunch one day, God drew the two of us together. God has used Scott's friendship to stretch me in my faith. From asking difficult questions, to expanding my love for the nations, Scott's love for Christ has been contagious.

Finally, meeting my future wife in college surely has been, next to my salvation, God's single greatest blessing to me. From early in our relationship, but especially in the crucible of marriage, I have learned more through her about God's love for me than through anyone else. Her biblical friendship toward me, in the best and worst of times, is a singular grace from God.

Writing this book has given me cause to evaluate and be encouraged in these and other biblical friendships. It has provided opportunities for gratitude, humility, and deep meditation on the grace friendship has been to me. It has also served as a convicting reminder that I am far from being the friend I should.

Nevertheless, each day brings fresh grace, and God is continually growing me in my pursuit of friendship. Because our biblical friendships flow from our shared relationship with Christ, he receives all the glory for their existence and fruitfulness. As God increases his grace to us through biblical friendships, each of us continues to grow in Christian unity.

Tim Keller writes that the kind of friendship I'm talking about is a "deep oneness" which occurs as each speaks the truth in love to each other and we "journey together to the same horizon."[54] What a wonderful reality! Biblical friendship comes with a shared horizon. We who have been saved by Jesus are all heading to the same destination—a place where the unity that Jesus prayed for in John 17 reaches its apex. Indeed, Keller goes on to say, "Spiritual friendship is the greatest journey of all, because the horizon is so high and far, yet sure—it is nothing less than 'the day of Jesus Christ' and what we will be like when we finally see him face-to-face."[55]

When I quoted Jesus' high-priestly prayer above, I stopped at verse 23. Now let's look at what Jesus says next: "Father, I desire that they also, whom you have given me, may be with me where I am, to see my glory that you have given me because you loved me before the foundation of the world" (John 17:24).

This prayer will be answered. We will be with Christ, where he is, seated in glory at the right hand of the Father. As Keller says, this is the horizon that all believers are traveling toward together.

In this book, we have seen that biblical friendships provide us with a tangible experience of the pre-existing unity in Christ that all Christians share—a unity which itself is a reflection of the perfect unity of the Trinity. That unity culminates, as Jesus prayed, in the wonder of our eternal future with him.

This means you and I are participants in the most epic of all possible dramas, a story with an inconceivably vast and profound story arc. That arc begins in eternity past, rising up from the perfect union of the Trinity. Somewhere in the middle, at the high point of the arc, Christians are miraculously caught up into the story line — and into God's pre-existing unity — through the redeeming and atoning work of Jesus Christ. The arc will come to rest when the Father grants the final and ultimate answer to Jesus' prayer in John 17:24. There, we will see with our eyes the glory the Father has given to Christ, a glory grounded in eternity-past love and union between the Father, Son, and Spirit.

The end of that story arc, just like the beginning, lasts forever.

Today, Christians are in the middle of the arc. In this time before the Lord's return, God is weaving a people into himself and into one another, with biblical friendship playing an essential role.

So this is what biblical friendship is and does. It gives us a way of experiencing and living out the fundamental drama of all creation. Fallen people are becoming joined to one another as an expression of our shared union with God. In the eternity hereafter with Jesus, this union will be essential to our joyful, worshipful productivity. At the end of the story arc, we *will* be with Jesus where he is, and we will see the glory God has given to him.

You and I, my Christian friend, are part of this infinitely wonderful story. Let's live it out while we are here. Through biblical friendship our shared lives can testify — within the church, and before a watching world — to the unity that comes from God himself.

Dig Deeper

1. Three aspects of cultivating unity in friendship are redeeming ordinary moments, practicing informal counseling, and embedded accountability. Where are you the strongest? Where are you the weakest?
2. Why is it so important that unity be a key component of biblical friendships?
3. Describe a time in your life when you've seen biblical friendship act as a witness to an unbelieving world.
4. Write down the names of two to three friends in your life. How can you grow in practically displaying the unity of the Trinity in these friendships?

Appendix

What else could I read on the topic of spiritual friendship?

Aelred of Rievaulx, *Spiritual Friendship*

Hugh Black, *Friendship*

Dietrich Bonhoeffer, *Life Together*

C.S. Lewis, *The Four Loves*

Augustine, *Confessions*

Sherry Turkle, *Alone Together* (secular source)

A.C. Grayling, *Friendship* (secular source)

Where do I begin the process of forging friendship?

Pray! I find this to be an underestimated step. Ask God to prepare you for biblical friendship, and then for wisdom in whom to pursue.

Look! Paul Miller writes, "Love begins with looking."[56] Who do you see? Who do you sit with on a Sunday morning? Who do you see at your local coffee shop? Who do you consistently cross paths with?

Follow through! Consistency of pursuit will be crucial to forming friendships. Too often, people begin with energy and good intentions, but then let things fall by the wayside. The friendship falls into a state of atrophy, pentant sin, I do believe the friend has a biblical obligation to speak the truth in love, confront, and follow through on the steps outlined in Matthew 18:15–17.[61]

How should I think about friendships with someone who struggles with same-sex attraction? How can we wisely guard our friendship from sin?

While we briefly touched on this in chapter five, there is still much more to be said on the topic. Homosexual orientation and same-sex attraction are not a part of God's original design and intention for humanity.[62] But where do you move from there? I believe friendship can be a primary means to deliver the good news of the gospel and its message of transformation to people who struggle.

Instead of moving away from them, what would it look like to come alongside and befriend them? David White of Harvest USA notes three unique challenges for the person who struggles with same-sex attraction as they approach friendship:[63]

1. It is not wise to pursue a close and intimate friendship with someone you find physically attractive.
2. Don't seek a best friend exclusively, but look to have a "larger base of relationships."
3. Cultivate a network of "multi-layered" friendships, where you can be known and loved. Multi-layered in terms of interests, pursuits, hobbies, and age.

It would be hard to improve on Ellen Dykas' excellent article[64] in the *Journal of Biblical Counseling* where she offers solid, biblical wisdom on this particular topic. A list of resources on this topic can be found on the website of the Biblical Counseling Coalition.[65]

What about boundaries in friendship?

This is a question that surfaces not only in discussions on friendship, but every other relational situation. In regards to friendship, the question typically gets framed thus, "I feel like my friend takes advantage of me sometimes or expects things from me unfairly. I think I need to set up some boundaries with them to protect me."

The language of boundaries[66] can mean different things for different people. I appreciate Ed Welch's wisdom on the topic where he writes, "The image of boundaries *describes* life in a fallen world more than *prescribes* it."[67] When the metaphor of a boundary is rightly employed, I believe it can help serve a good purpose (e.g., a wife in an abusive relationship should have some type of boundary in place).

In friendship, the concept of boundaries often feeds our desire for self-protection, isolation, and comfortable living, and an exemption from self-sacrificial love. All of which goes against the message of the gospel, and friendship in particular.

Welch concludes his helpful article, "When boundaries become a lifestyle, we are going to think about self-protection more than love. The overarching image is that we should break down boundaries between ourselves and others rather than erect them."[68] After all it is Jesus who enters and enfolds us into his life, rather than erecting boundaries to exclude us.

Author

Jonathan Holmes serves at Parkside Church in Cleveland, Ohio as the Pastor of Counseling. He graduated with degrees in Biblical Counseling and History from The Master's College and a master's degree from Trinity Evangelical Divinity School. Jonathan and his wife, Jennifer, are parents of three beautiful daughters, Ava, Riley, and Ruby. Jonathan also serves on the Council Board of the Biblical Counseling Coalition.

Endnotes

1. Kevin DeYoung, "The Gift of Friendship and the Godliness of Good Friends (Part 1)," July 5, 2011, http://thegospelcoalition.org/blogs/kevindeyoung/2011/07/05/the-gift-of-friendship-and-the-godliness-of-good-friends-part-1/ .

2. *The Westminster Confession of Faith*, chapter 2, section 3: In the unity of the Godhead there be three Persons of one substance, power, and eternity: God the Father, God the Son, and God the Holy Ghost. The Father is of none, neither begotten nor proceeding; the Son is eternally begotten of the Father; the Holy Ghost eternally proceeding from the Father and the Son.

3. R. Kent Hughes, *Disciplines of a Godly Man* (Wheaton, IL: Crossway Books, 2001), 58.

4. This quote is from a Tim Keller sermon, March 1, 1998- Spiritual Friendship from Acts 20:36-21:8. Link to the sermon is available here: http://www.gospelinlife.com/spiritual-friendship-6712.html

5. Hugh Black, *Friendship* (Ontario, Canada: Joshua Press, 1898), 35.

6. Indeed, two verses later, Adam shamelessly tries to dump all the blame on Eve.

7. Rusty McKie, "Some Things Are Worth Dying For," http://cbmw.org/men/manhood/some-things-are-worth-dying-for/, (Accessed March 21, 2014).

8. Augustine, *Confessions* (London: Penguin Books, 1961), 75.

9. Aelred of Rievaulx, *Spiritual Friendship* (Kalamazoo, MI: Cistercian Publications, 1974), 74.

10. Tim Keller, *The Meaning of Marriage* (New York, NY: Dutton, 2011), 114.

11. Sherry Turkle, *Alone Together: Why We Expect More from Technology and Less from Each Other* (New York, NY: Basic Books, 2011), 1.

12. "Estimates from epidemiological studies indicate that Major Depression afflicts about 10% of adults in the United States each year, and nearly a fifth of the population at some point in their lives." Allan V. Horwitz & Jerome C. Wakefield, *The Lost of Sadness: How Psychiatry Transformed Normal Sorrow into a Depressive Disorder* (New York, NY: Oxford University Press, 2007), 4.

13. Sherry Turkle, "The Flight From Conversation," April 21, 2012, http://www.nytimes.com/2012/04/22/opinion/sunday/the-flight-from-conversation.html?pagewanted=all.

14. Nicholas Tufnell, "Happy Birthday Facebook, you made me a nervous wreck," February 4, 2014, http://www.wired.co.uk/news/archive/2014-02/04/facebook-made-me-a-nervous-wreck.
15. Turkle, *Alone Together*, 1.
16. Paul Tripp and Tim Lane, *Relationships: A Mess Worth Making* (Greensboro, NC: New Growth Press, 2006), 18.
17. Jonathan Safran Foer, "How Not To Be Alone," June 8, 2013, http://www.nytimes.com/2013/06/09/opinion/sunday/how-not-to-be-alone.html.
18. Dietrich Bonhoeffer, *Life Together* (San Francisco, CA: Harper & Row, 1954), 21.
19. C.S. Lewis, *The Four Loves* (Boston, Massachusetts: Mariner Books, 2012), 66.
20. Tim Keller, "Friendship," http://sermons.redeemer.com/store/index.cfm?fuseaction=product.display&product_ID=18432&ParentCat=6.
21. William Arnot, *Studies in Proverbs* (Grand Rapids, MI: Kregel Publications, 1978), 380.
22. Tolkien, J.R.R., (New York: Mariner Books, 2004), 105.
23. Richard Baxter, *The Reformed Pastor* (Carlisle, PA: Banner of Truth Trust, 1974), 118.
24. Charles Bridges, *Proverbs* (Carlisle, Pennsylvania: Banner of Truth Trust, 1968), 505.
25. William Deresiewicz, "Faux Friendship," December 6, 2009, https://chronicle.com/article/Faux-Friendship/49308/.
26. Tim Keller, "Why You Can't See Your Biggest Flaws" accessed from the The Gospel Coalition, http://thegospelcoalition.org/article/why-you-cant-see-your-biggest-flaws. Accessed 7/29/14.
27. R. Kent Hughes, *Disciplines of a Godly Man* (Wheaton, IL: Crossway Books, 2001), 62.
28. Tim Challies, "The Myself I was Yesterday," February 5, 2014, http://www.challies.com/christian-living/the-myself-i-was-yesterday.
29. Carolinne White, *Christian Friendship in the Fourth Century* (Cambridge University Press, 2002), 62.
30. Michael Haykin, "With A Little Help From My Friends" accessed from the 9Marks website, http://www.9marks.org/journal/little-help-my-friends. Accessed 7/29/14
31. C.S. Lewis, *The Four Loves* (Boston, Massachusetts: Mariner Books, 2012), 64.
32. Ibid, 65
33. Augustine, *Letters*, 258

34. Ibid

35. Augustine quoted in *Friendship* by A.C. Grayling (New Haven, CT:Yale University Press), 67-68.

36. Frost, Robert. *Mountain Interval* (NewYork: Henry Holt and Company, 1920), Bartleby.com, 1999.

37. Tim Chester, *A Meal With Jesus: Discovering Grace, Community, & Mission Around the Table* (Wheaton, Illinois: Crossway Publishers, 2011), 46.

38. Ibid, 47.

39. Augustine, *Confessions*, Book IV, 77-78.

40. Rusty McKie, "Some Things Are Worth Dying For," http://cbmw.org/men/manhood/some-things-are-worth-dying-for/. (Accessed 21 March 2014).

41. Blaise Pascal, *Pensées*, Section 3, 101.

42. Hugh Black, 39.

43. C.S. Lewis, *The Four Loves* (Boston, Massachusetts: Mariner Books, 2012), 60.

44. Additional counsel is offered on this topic in the Appendix.

45. Wesley Hill's nomenclature here of "gay and lesbian Christians" can be easily misunderstood. For a full explanation of the phraseology see, *Washed &Waiting: Reflections on Christian Faithfulness and Homosexuality* (Grand Rapids, MI: Zondervan, 2010). His larger point, however, is that friendship offers a unique opportunity for the struggler to repent, turn to Christ daily in his weakness, and have his/her desires changed by the gospel as he/she lives faithfully in the midst of Christian community and friendship.

46. Wesley Hill, "The Problem of Gay Friendship," January 6, 2014, http://theotherjournal.com/2014/01/06/the-problem-of-gay-friendship/.

47. Again this topic cannot be fully developed here. I realize there are opportunities where meaningful friendships can become an ensnaring temptation for the SSA struggle. However, I would regret that possibility would rob others of taking meaningful steps towards building intimate friendships.

48. Aelred of Rievaulx, *Spiritual Friendship* (Kalamazoo, MI: Cistercian Publications, 1974), 71.

49. I am not overlooking the centrality of marriage in God's plan to demonstrate to the world the relationship of Christ and the church.To the contrary, biblical friendship will necessarily be a central component of any strong Christian marriage.

50. Jay Pathak and Dave Runyon, *The Art of Neighboring* (Grand

Rapids, MI: Baker Books, 2012), 94.

51. An excellent book on this topic is PaulTripp's, *Instruments in the Redeemer's Hands*.

52. Dick Lucas, *John* (London, England: Christian Focus Publications, 1999), 205.

53. RalphWaldo Emerson, "Essay IV Friendship," http://www.emersoncentral.com/friendship.htm.

54. Tim Keller, *The Meaning of Marriage* (NewYork, NY: Dutton, 2011), 116-117.

55. Tim Keller, *The Meaning of Marriage* (NewYork, NY: Dutton, 2011), 117.

56. Paul Miller, *Love Walked Among Us: Learning to Love Like Jesus* (Colorado Springs, CO: NavPress, 2001), 33.

57. For more on the topic of realistic expectation in marriage, I'd recommend Margaret and Dwight Peterson's book, *Are You Waiting for "The One"?: Cultivating Realistic, Positive Expectations for Christian Marriage* (Downers Grove, IL: IVP Books, 2011).

58. For more on this topic, I'd recommend Joel R. Beeke, *Friends and Lovers: Cultivating Companionship and Intimacy in Marriage* (Cruciform Press, 2012).

59. Hugh Black, *Friendship* (Ontario, Canada: Joshua Press, 1898), 71.

60. cf. Matthew 5:21-24, 18:21-35, Mark 11:25, Luke 17:1-4

61. 1 Corinthians 15:33, Galatians 6:1-3, Ephesians 5:11

62. Wesley Hill writes of homosexuality that it is indeed "a tragic sign that human nature and relationships are fractured by sin." (Wesley Hill, *Washed and Waiting* [Grand Rapids, MI: Zondervan, 2010],15.)

63. DavidWhite, *Can You Change IfYou're Gay?* (Greensboro, NC: New Growth Press, 2013), 18-19.

64. Ellen Dykas, "Close Friends or Entangled Hearts? Joys and Dangers inWoman-to-Woman Friendships," *Journal of Biblical Counseling,*Winter 2006. 24-28.

65. Top 24 Resources on Same-Sex Attraction: http://biblicalcounselingcoalition.org/books/lists/24-top-resources-on-same-sex-attraction.

66. Boundaries is a concept popularized by Henry Cloud and John Townsend in, *Boundaries: When to SayYes, How to Say No to Take Control ofYour Life* (Grand Rapids, MI: Zondervan, 1992).

67. EdWelch, "Boundaries in Relationships," *Journal of Biblical Counseling,* Spring 2004. 18. (emphasis in the original)

68. Ibid, 24.

bit.ly/Srvnt

Servanthood as Worship
The Privilege of Life in a Local Church

by Nate Palmer

**We [serve] because he first
[served] us. –1 John 1:19 [sort of]**

**What ever happened to servant-
hood? Here is a biblical presenta-
tion of our calling to serve in the
church, motivated by the grace
that is ours in the gospel.**

"In an age where the church can be likened to Cinderella—beautiful,
but largely ignored and forgotten—Nate Palmer's brief book forces
us to rethink both the church and our relationship to her. In an age
where egocentrism ensures we sing, 'O say, can you see—what's in
it for me?' on a weekly basis, Palmer forces us to say instead, 'How
can I best serve the church?' Looking at the needs of others rather
than one's own is possibly the most serious deficiency in the church
today. Reading this book will help redress the deficiency. I heartily
recommend it."
Derek W.H. Thomas, Professor of Theology, Reformed
Theological Seminary (Jackson)

"Think of these pages as a handbook. It contains a sustainable, practical vision for serving in the local church that is powered by grace.
Along the way, you'll get a mini theological education."
Justin Buzzard, pastor, San Francisco Bay Area, Buzzard Blog

"In our media-crazed, me-first culture, the art of the basin and the
towel has been shoved off onto those who get paid to serve—
certainly a call to serve in humility can't be God's will for all of us, or
could it? Nate Palmer gets at the heart of our resistance.. I strongly
recommend this book."
Elyse Fitzpatrick, author of Because He Loves Me

bit.ly/WHOAMI

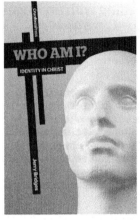

Who Am I?
Identity in Christ

by Jerry Bridges

**Jerry Bridges unpacks Scripture
to give the Christian eight clear,
simple, interlocking answers to
one of the most essential
questions of life.**

"Jerry Bridges' gift for simple but deep spiritual communication is fully
displayed in this warm-hearted, biblical spelling out of the Christian's
true identity in Christ."

> **J. I. Packer, *Theological Editor,* ESV Study Bible; *author,*
> Knowing God, A Quest for Godliness, Concise Theology**

"I know of no one better prepared than Jerry Bridges to write *Who
Am I?* He is a man who knows who he is in Christ and he helps us to
see succinctly and clearly who we are to be. Thank you for another
gift to the Church of your wisdom and insight in this book."

> **R.C. Sproul, *founder, chairman, president, Ligonier Ministries;
> executive editor,* Tabletalk *magazine; general editor,* The
> Reformation Study Bible**

"*Who Am I?* answers one of the most pressing questions of our time
in clear gospel categories straight from the Bible. This little book is a
great resource to ground new believers and remind all of us of what
God has made us through faith in Jesus. Thank the Lord for Jerry
Bridges, who continues to provide the warm, clear, and biblically
balanced teaching that has made him so beloved to this generation
of Christians."

> **Richard D. Phillips, *Senior Minister, Second Presbyterian
> Church, Greenville, SC***

bit.ly/CPWrestle

Wrestling with an Angel
A Story of Love, Disability
and the Lessons of Grace

by Greg Lucas

**The riveting, inspiring true story
that readers have called
"a touchstone book of my life,"
and "alternately hilarious and
heartbreaking," a book that
"turns the diamond of grace in
such a way that you see facets
you never really noticed before."**

"C.S. Lewis wrote that he paradoxically loved *The Lord of the Rings* because it 'broke his heart'—and Greg Lucas' writing does the same for me."
Justin Taylor, Managing Editor, ESV Study Bible

"Witty... stunning... striking... humorous and heartfelt. *Wrestling with an Angel* provides a fresh, honest look at one father's struggle to embrace God in the midst of his son's disability. Can sheer laughter and weeping gracefully coexist in a world of so much affliction? Greg knows all about it. I highly recommend this wonderfully personal book!"
Joni Eareckson Tada, Joni and Friends International

"You will laugh; you will cry. You will feel sick; you will feel inspired. You will be repulsed by the ugliness of sin; you will be overwhelmed by the love of God. Greg Lucas takes us on an unforgettable ride as he extracts the most beautiful insights into grace from the most painful experiences of life."
David P. Murray, Puritan Reformed Theological Seminary

"Greg Lucas is a captivating storyteller. When he writes about life with Jake, I recognize God's grace and loving persistence in my life. I want more!"
Noël Piper, author, and wife of pastor and author John Piper

Friends and Lovers
Cultivating Companionship and
Intimacy in Marriage

by Joel R. Beeke

Marriage is for God's glory and our good.

The secret?

Intimate Christian companionship.

"A book about love, marriage, and sex from Joel Beeke that is surprisingly candid yet without a trace of smuttiness. Fresh and refreshingly straightforward, this is the best book of its kind."
Derek W H Thomas, Visiting Professor, Reformed Theo. Sem.

"Marriage is hard work. And wonderful. And sometimes, it's both at the same time. *Friends and Lovers* is like a personal mentoring session on marriage with a man whose heart is devoted to seeing Christ honored in how we love each other as husbands and wives. It's full of practical wisdom and grace. A delight."
Bob Lepine, Co-Host, FamilyLife Today

"By laying the theological, emotional, social, and spiritual foundations of marriage before heading to the bedroom, Joel Beeke provides a healthy corrective to the excessive and obsessive sex-focus of our generation and even of some pastors. But, thankfully, he also goes on to provide wise, practical, down-to-earth direction for couples wanting to discover or recover physical intimacy that will both satisfy themselves and honor God."
Dr. David Murray, Professor, Puritan Reformed Theo. Sem.

"There is no better book than this to renew the affection of happy marriage."
Geoffrey Thomas, Pastor, Alfred Place Baptist Church, Wales

bit.ly/Christ-in

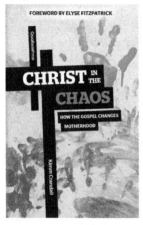

Christ in the Chaos
How the Gospel Changes
Motherhood

by Kimm Crandall

MOMS: Stop comparing yourself to others. Stop striving to meet false expectations. Stop thinking your performance dictates your worth.

Look to the gospel for rest, joy, sufficiency, identity, and motivation.

"Although Kimm Crandall's message would revive any soul longing for the breath of the gospel of grace, I am especially eager to recommend this book to that heart who strives to know God and to make him known to the little ones who call her 'Momma.' Kimm is a candid and gracious fellow sojourner, faithfully pointing to God's immeasurable steadfast love and grace in the midst of our mess."

> *Lauren Chandler, wife of Matt Chandler (pastor of The Village Church), mother of three, writer, singer, and speaker*

"What an amazingly wild and wise, disruptive and delighting, freeing and focusing book. Kimm's book is for every parent willing to take the stewardship of children and the riches of the gospel seriously. This is one of the most helpful and encouraging books on parenting I've read in the past twenty years. This will be a book you will want to give to parents, to-be parents, and grandparents."

> *Scotty Smith, author; Founding Pastor, Christ Community Church*

"Kimm Crandall has discovered that chaos can be the perfect context in which to experience God's liberating grace. She is a wise, practical, gospel-drenched guide for anyone navigating through the wearisome terrain of parenting."

> *Tullian Tchividjian, author; Pastor, Coral Ridge Presbyterian Church*

CPSIA information can be obtained at www.ICGtesting.com
Printed in the USA
BVOW09s2021101114

374486BV00003B/7/P